A. Thinker: Your Very Own Swift Kick in the Ass!

A Survival Guide for Real Estate Investment, the Stock Market, and Other People's Self-Indulgence

J. L. WILLIAMS

ISBN:1-4839-1817-3
ISBN 13: 978-1-4839-1817-4

Library of Congress Control Number: 2013905439
CreateSpace Independent Publishing Platform
North Charleston, South Carolina

Printed in the USA

This publication is designed to provide accurate and reliable
information with regard to the subject matter covered. It is
sold with the understanding that the publisher is not engaged
in rendering legal, financial, or other professional advice.
Laws and practices often vary from state to state and if
legal or other expert assistance is required, the services of a
competent professional should be sought.

It takes talent—and will—to attain success. Luck is only a factor, and a comparatively minor one.

—Nicolas Darvas, world famous dancer and
self-taught investor

If you do not work passionately (even furiously) at being the best in the world at what you do, you fail your talent, your destiny, and your god.

—George Lois

What we do not call education is more precious than that which we call so. We form no guess, at the time of receiving a thought, of its comparative value. And education often wastes its effort in attempts to thwart and balk this natural magnetism, which is sure to select what belongs to it.

—Ralph Waldo Emerson

ACKNOWLEDGEMENTS

A book doesn't get published without a group of brilliant and talented people to bring it to fruition. First of all, thanks to Travis Craine and the project team at CreateSpace for their expertise and knowledge of publishing. And a huge thanks to Laura, the editor assigned to my book project. This book would have been bloated and without purpose if not for your revisions and suggestions.

Thanks to my gracious parents for investing in me and my dreams and for teaching me how to be rich without the need for a bunch of zeros in my bank account. To both my sisters, thanks for putting up with my crap and stubbornness, and to my younger sister who encouraged the idea for the "swift kick in the ass" part of the title—I appreciate the brilliant feedback. Thanks to the Creator for keeping me safe all these years, and for all the lessons I've had to learn along the way.

I extend my sincerest appreciation to the Internet, Wikipedia, Google, and Yahoo! for their extensive resourcefulness. I should also thank the fantastic professionals that made my real estate search and purchase much easier: David Keenum, John McNichol and the many others I have forgotten by name. You guys are the best! To anyone who has given a helping hand with the renovations on my house and/or spread a word of encouragement while I put this project together—Timothy Davis, Ryan Wilson, Kelly Williams, Andy Thoss, Stephen Talbert, Jarred Jackson, and Steve Frantz. Thanks for bringing kindling to the fire beneath my feet.

Most importantly, I want to give a **BIG** thanks to all my readers for purchasing this book and contributing a portion to the value of my current flip project. This is for you, so please enjoy!

CONTENTS

FOREWORD

I have read that most novels and books are really letters written with one person in mind. There is some element of truth to that statement, at least for me. The idea for this book was the good swift kick in the ass I needed to get motivated. I had to do something. I was sick of waiting for the "right moment" to write a book.

The other reason I wrote the book was for those people who have big dreams and high aspirations to be something better in this life and are looking for ways to achieve it. This is for their kindred souls and minds. I hope this finds you well, wherever you happen to be.

Furthermore, I understand that all of us come from different backgrounds and have our own unique set of circumstances to deal with. This is, however, not an excuse for a lack of financial education. I wrote this book specifically for a special and elite group of people (I'm talking about you genius!) and hereby dedicate it to you.

Here are the things I went ahead and assumed about you fine individuals, given that you picked this book out for yourself and not someone else (altruism is a virtue):

⇨ You desire financial security and control over your life

⇨ You are willing to do whatever it takes to achieve that goal

⇨ You are constantly seeking education to enrich your life and others

⇨ You can see the larger picture and purpose for your life

⇨ You are capable of doing simple mathematics

⇨ You can operate a computer, including the Internet

I would also love to add the value of positive thinking to that list, although some of the most negative moments in my life have led to some of the greatest discoveries and creations. So maybe there is a benefit to negativity after all?

Another thing—the younger you are, the more time you have to become rooted in the principles for wealth. If I had one thing I could give to myself when I was just starting out as a young adult in the vast and evolving marketplace, it would be this book. Maybe I could have seen the larger picture and took action to bring it closer to my grasp.

P.S. Before we get to the good stuff, I want to let you know I am self publishing this book, meaning that I am allowed creative control over what I share with you in these pages. I could very well tell you that aliens exist and are preparing to extract our resources (you know, the *renewable* ones?)

For fiction this might possibly work. Non-fiction though? Hell no. Not a chance. My happy ass had better tell the truth, so help me God. Keeping this in mind, here it is folks: the tell-all (most anyways) of my polygamous affair with money, success, and personal finance.

I. Backstory

I am a firm believer in the people. If given the truth, they can be depended upon to meet any national crisis. The great point is to bring them the real facts.

—Abraham Lincoln

Once Upon a Time…Wait This Isn't A Fairy Tale!

2005. The year I graduated high school. At that time, I didn't have a clue what I was going to do with my life and not much of a financial plan to guide my path along the way. I did what most of the other smart kids did: applied for financial aid and went to college the year following graduation. Major? Ehhhhh…undecided. My student ID retorted that I was a bachelor of the arts and sciences and I came to like that classification much better.

Roll the clocks forward to 2013. I'm not a millionaire (yet, anyway) but I have a definite plan to become one. After I read Napoleon Hill's book *Think and Grow Rich* (which I quote from time to time), I set the goal of becoming a millionaire by June 25, 2014. That was exactly three years from the date I wrote my definiteness of purpose, as stated in his book—which was written in 1937 and still applies today. Do yourself a solid and check it out.

Although I'm not rich yet, I know that my dream will soon become a reality. After all, attaining wealth isn't something that just happens overnight. It takes time and unwavering commitment.

My personal plan involves investing in real estate and flipping it for profit, along with a few carefully selected stock-market investments and this book, plus any others I write that can provide value in other people's lives, whether that be for informative or entertainment purposes. These are the streams of passive income I've designated for my life. Hopefully these examples and some of the others in this book can work for yours. This is why you're here, right?

I bought a house with a twenty percent down payment before I was twenty-five years old. Although that's not a grandiose accomplishment, it is one achieved by few people in their early twenties. I had everything I needed to put a book together and every reason to make it entertaining as possible.

I've been in construction trades since I was seventeen years old (residential and commercial cabinetry, painting, insulation, maintenance) and I've learned a lot, giving me an advantage in flipping houses without hiring expensive contractors. I always tackle every project firsthand, even if I don't know how. I'll hit up YouTube for tutorials or ask somebody who's been in construction for a lifetime.

Sometime around May of 2008, I was twenty-one years old and working a construction job, getting paid nine dollars an hour and living in the spare bedroom of my parents' house. After the weekends rolled by and Monday morning greeted my sober face, I usually found myself broke and struggled through the week until Friday's glorious paycheck cleared the bank.

I also carried with me a string of bad habits—overspending, eating out all the time, excessive drinking, and cigarette smoking—that didn't help my situation. I was sick and tired of my life. I could never seem to get ahead financially. What I needed was a much stronger foundation upon which to build my personal financial freedom plan.

I knew I would never acquire much by making a measly nine dollars an hour. My talents were worth much more than that, even if I was the only person to acknowledge them. Between 2006 and 2008, my self-discovery led to a lot of changes in my life, and I heard a lot of talk about how people were making money through real estate investment.

The housing bubble and credit crisis that happened between 2007 and 2009 made many Americans realize they had bought and borrowed at the worst possible time. I remember the news had ordained it the subprime mortgage crisis as if to make it sound anything less than a blatant fiasco.

The financial markets tanked, banks and other lenders closed their doors or merged with other firms, the government began buying up junk mortgages and other toxic assets (remember Fannie Mae and Freddie Mac anyone?), unemployment became rampant as people were laid off left and right, and the foreclosure tally grew by the day. Lending institutions and big corporations were swiftly issued bailouts, leaving the American taxpayers to foot the bill.

Home prices and property values continued to drop into 2011 and 2012 as more people foreclosed or filed for bankruptcy. Who knows how far these government choices will extend into our future years? Of course, the banks and government aren't the only ones to blame.

What about the folks who bought the overpriced homes with little or no money down and took out second and third mortgages to buy boats, new vehicles, or…wait a second. More homes with no money down? Did they think that could last without incomes to match their financial responsibilities?

I knew I needed to be smarter than the majority and realize the buying opportunities around me. Supply flourished and demand came to a screeching halt, leading to almost rock-bottom pricing as banks were hungry to sell properties and remove them from their liabilities list and into the assets category—the sooner the better in a falling market.

I worked with a guy who had previously worked on an oil rig, and we talked in-depth about his offshore adventures. I was curious and asked a lot of questions, and he was generous in sharing his story with me. He got his first taste of offshore life while working on a crew boat for a company that was relatively close to where I lived at the time.

One afternoon after work, I found the company's office and filled out an application for employment. I was green as holy hell but I didn't care. I figured I needed one chance to prove myself to these people and I would be in like Flynn. Let me say that I was *committed* to the task of getting a job with them. I called the home office every week, sometimes two and three times. I wanted them to be so sick of hearing my voice that they would finally see if I could learn the ropes.

This went on for four to six weeks until, finally, someone from the human resources department told me to come in for my safety training, drug screen, and physical. The first few nights will either make you or break you out there. All I needed to see was those first few checks and my mind was made up: $585.68, $837.55, $1,230.26. Small potatoes to some, but really who cares? I *felt* rich inside and that emotional charge came way of me changing my environment and circumstances.

When I awoke the next morning, a Friday morning I remember well, I called the boss directly and quit my job over the phone. Instantaneous freedom never felt so great! He asked me if it was my thirty-second notice. Ha! I replied with, "Yeah, something like that," and hung up. I don't like being a jackass, but the opportunity had come up, and I wouldn't let anything hold me back from my goal.

I worked on utility boats and crew boats in the Gulf of Mexico for the next two years. My schedule for most hitches out was fourteen days on the boat, and then seven days off. That didn't give me a lot of time to spend money or get stupid. Luckily, I have the greatest parents in the world, who never asked me to pay rent or anything else (just asked I pay my own debts), and I accumulated money more quickly than I could spend it.

The first thing I did was pay off my debts—auto loans, college loans, outstanding late fees at the library, and so on. By mid-2010 I wanted to come ashore and find a house to buy and then flip. While offshore, I had read several books on real estate foreclosures, flipping, and investing. Not to mention our fine government was giving away a credit for first-time home buyers of up to eight thousand dollars.

I had saved over twenty-three thousand dollars in my bank account—and that's after paying for some hefty mistakes I had made along the way. I found a land job—construction once again—and visited the library regularly for more books on investment and personal success.

When I finally squared my credit problem away in early 2011, I obtained preapproval for an eighty thousand dollar mortgage—I live on the Gulf Coast, where the average mortgage is around one hundred and seventeen thousand dollars—and was progressing toward my goal of becoming a full-time real estate investor.

I looked for houses according to the plan I lay out in Chapter VII. Every day after work I looked at properties online for anything of value. I probably visited thirty-five to fifty houses and made offers on several of those to get the feel for bidding. Just wait until you see multiple buyers interested in purchasing one property. Watch out—a bidding war's about to commence! If you're the seller, this is a dream come true.

I found the house I had been looking for after about five months of scouting the area. It had just come on the market and was uglier than homemade sin inside. Sponge-painted maroon walls in the living room, yellow-and-maroon stripes in the kitchen, popcorn-textured ceilings, hole through the foyer wall and the adjacent bedroom where a fish tank used to sit, outdated 1980s linoleum, concrete floors, and stained carpet. It was perfect!

I was beat to the bid. Sometimes banks won't entertain another bid while they are reviewing or approving an offer. When I found out I was beaten to the bank with a higher bid, I was heartbroken. I thought that the house was really the one, my own diamond in the rough. But I went back home, got on the Zillow website, and started my search again.

About a week later, my realtor called me up at work to tell me the deal on the house fell through, meaning somebody wasn't properly prepared for go time. I had my guns loaded. We submitted my initial offer and the bank agreed to it. I put twenty percent down on the house and took over the property two months before my twenty-fifth birthday.

Before I bought this house, I had a plan for it. I could picture the color schemes, see the crown molding already hanging on the wall, and knew what it would take to make the property shine above the others on the market. I wrote my plan out on a poster board and its resting place is on my bedroom wall, where it cannot be avoided.

I know that if I can picture something in my imagination, then it can be done—and if I can't do it, then someone else has done it before me. Possibly, hopefully, someone's written a book or recorded a video tutorial—something that will help my efforts in achieving whatever I set out to do.

It is our duty to serve others and help them achieve their own dreams and goals. If you can provide enough value and service by doing that, you may find your bank account complements your involvement, and that will free up your precious time to pursue your wildest dreams and endeavors.

What are *my* wildest dreams and goals? To live my life as a full-time investor—mostly in residential real estate and also, but not limited to, stocks, people, education, businesses, ideas, dreams, passions, guitars, and muscle cars. I enjoy taking that which is unkind to the eye and making it beautiful and unique—much like a sculptor takes a chunk of ordinary rock and hammers away at it until he molds an intricate statue with his craftsmanship.

What I am trying to achieve with this book is to help and educate teens and young adults about the real world and the business world—albeit in a humorous way. I approached this book as though we are having a one-on-one conversation someplace comfortable—on the beach, in your favorite chair, or chatting by the fireplace over beer, if ye be of age that is.

We can laugh with each other and make wisecracks because we're friends and fellow travelers on this highway to financial freedom. Most importantly, I want you to think more in-depth about the things that surround your everyday life. Be a true American thinker and opportunist.

In case you're curious about the title, I was going to title this book *American Thinker*. I nonchalantly shortened the title one evening when I e-mailed the introduction to a friend, and the idea grew on me. It seemed to inspire more thought on your part.

How many adjectives start with the letter *A* that can accurately describe your thinking? Amazing, astute, adventurous, applicable, adamant, astounding, ardent, accelerated, attractive, aberrant, audacious? Just not archaic, average, or asinine, OK?

I hope I can help solve some of your problems and broaden your mind with my ideas and experiences about financial freedom that are marinated with a sarcastic undertone. I have included an example of my own real estate purchase agreement and estimated closing costs sheet at the back of this book for informative purposes. I wanted to give you a visual of some of the terms and quoted prices for those miscellaneous things you don't always hear or read about.

You'll see many things on these sheets that I haven't mentioned in the book because I don't have a long technical definition for each and quite frankly most of it is ungodly boring for the capacity of this book, but you can find a smorgasbord of helpful knowledge over at www.investopedia. com.

Of all the different books on personal finance, investing, and success I've read, I can't remember reading a book like the one I have created. It isn't in-depth about investing techniques or formulas, but I hope you'll be able to pull a golden nugget out of these pages for your own benefit.

Here's a toast to the fulfillment of your dreams, and may your life be prosperous for all your days. Now, if I can just get you to sit still while I attempt to ignite the huge pile of lint in your qualitative brain.

II. QUESTIONS TO ASK

YOURSELF

I speak my mind freely on all things, even on those which perhaps exceed my capacity and which I by no means hold to be within my jurisdiction. And so the opinion I give of them is to declare the measure of my sight, not the measure of things.

—Michel de Montaigne

Love at First Sight: A. Thinker Meets A. Planner, Which Leads To the Birth of A. Action-Taker

What strikes us to conjure up certain memories, think about past lives, have wickedly vivid dreams, or remember important figures in our lives such as our spouses, parents, siblings, or best friends? What causes us to throw our financial control out the window or accept and settle for mediocrity or maintain routines and habits that do not pay any dividends or returns?

Why have all these distractions? Why can't we focus our attention on creating the life we've always imagined? I think everyone would appreciate keeping their lives simple and living out their years in comfortable fashion. Comfortable does not necessarily mean rich and comfortable. You can sacrifice comfort today for a supremely more comfortable life in—depending on your speed of execution and the passion behind it—a few short years. They will fly by anyway, right? So make the absolute best return on your time. After all, time is limited and clearly your most prized asset.

Of course, most people aspire to living the American Dream. Do any of these goals either apply to you, or do you aspire to any of them? Note the sarcasm, please.

⇨ Good job (Yay! I'm safe and secure! And usually broke. How did this happen?)

⇨ Great benefits (Would you check out that dental plan!)

⇨ Nice home in American suburbia (We just bought a house in Exorbitant Elms subdivision and we only had to put down 3% of our own money!)

⇨ Brand new ride ($30,000!! What a steal! No credit—No problem! We'll have you behind the wheel of a new car today! Just sign and drive!)

⇨ Superb companionship (Why don't Marsha and you come join us? We're all going out for cocktails later and we can discuss the trivialities of our American lives!)

⇨ Super-duper kids (Straight-*A* students, voted Most Likely to Succeed, Valedictorians, and world-class chess players. Star athletes too, what the hell. Might as well make it good while we're here!)

⇨ 401(k) package (Thought process=Ballin! You are smart to be saving for your future. Let's be perfectly honest with ourselves though, and admit we probably don't have a damn clue what we're invested in. All we know is that educated businessmen dressed in iron clad suits have it under control for us.)

Choices = The Reason You Are Where You're At

That's just a short list. It could go on and on. I wouldn't dare deny the advantages of each item on the list. What I want you to think about is whether this list reflects what *you* want to achieve, or is it a picture painted on someone else's canvas?

Everyone in your personal life has an idea of who you are, an image they attribute to you, detailing their perception of both your interior and exterior qualities. They like to think they know you well, but do they know your true potential, your talents and ambitions, your passions and burning desires?

Ask yourself the most important question of all: What do *you* want the most from life? Stop for a minute and really contemplate it. What makes your mind do somersaults at the thought of? Think about the feelings you generate when you imagine yourself indulging in this action, whatever it may be. Your *desire* is a powerful and sovereign emotion and one of the greatest tools in your arsenal.

Think about sex for a moment. Throws the switch on the memory and the imagination, doesn't it? Imagine that you can channel that desire or sex emotion of yours. Yes, you control whatever traffic passes through your mental passageways. You operate the dams and control the locks for the ships passing through. Everyday, you make the decisions and choices that will shape the course of the rest of your life. I know that's a deep subject and not one easily understood by shallow minds.

Maybe your dream is simple: you want to live in a nice home in a nice neighborhood. Make the dream specific. Do you want a brick home in a nice and upcoming subdivision, or would you rather have a three-bedroom, two-bath brick home with a stone fireplace, walk-in showers, and custom granite countertops that sits comfortably on a ten-acre lot in a private, gated subdivision with a stocked lake and a custom-built boat launch?

The mind loves specifics. Visualize your dream down to the last detail. Get out there and find what you want. Instigate your creative side and construct a collage of what success means for you. Hang it in your bedroom or wherever you will see it the most. Hell, take a seat in the boss's chair for a change if your aspiration is to be the head of the company you work for.

The question to ask yourself is: To what lengths would you go to reach your goals? How willing are you to achieve your goals and how badly do you want them? What price would you pay to make it to the other side of your imagination and actually manifest your dreams into tangible form?

Why do you want to achieve this goal so badly? The answer to that question is the fuel for the fire burning beneath you desire. Maybe you want to retire early in life and focus on your real dreams, let's say between the ages of thirty to thirty-five. Wait a second…you don't think that's possible? It is. There are thousands of success stories that can aid you in ascertaining this fact. You've got to find the people who are doing it now or have done it in the past. Ever heard of Google?

Perhaps you have put together a plan to raise five million dollars and donate it to a St. Jude Children's Research Hospital in your area. Maybe you want to make sure your family is taken care of in the future. The *why* needs enough power and emotion behind it to get your ass in high gear, even if you don't "feel like it." Do it anyway—it's called willpower for a reason.

Conditioning 101: Elimination of Doubt and Fear With an Emphasis on Finding a Greater Purpose

Keep progressing and moving forward with your plans and goals. Cast aside any doubts and fears! They are the holes in your vessel, capable of sinking all you have worked so hard for. See yourself winning and know, without a doubt, that you will achieve the goal you have imagined. Play out scenarios in your mind every day of achieving this feat in whatever way, however silly it may seem or how far-fetched it sounds to you at the time. If you don't consistently feed your desire and direct your mind toward your goal, then life will serve you more of the same shit you've been getting.

Make a goal, set a definite purpose or life intention that you aspire to and write it down so you can read it over every day. Think of it as a mission statement that is created to align your thoughts and beliefs with what you want the most from life. Accept no excuses from yourself or from anyone else for not making strides toward this goal every day.

Give ideas life by employing faith and hope so they may live on. Here's a simple example that has been tailored for a budding real estate investor. As Sherlock Holmes would say: Elementary, my dear Watson!

I intend to acquire $1,000,000 dollars by January 1, 2014. In return for this money, I will give my time and do more than what I am paid for in the job I seek or entrepreneurial path I choose to follow. This will fund my real estate investments as well as any other investment vehicle I believe will yield me high dividends and income.

All the while, I will continue to further my education and invest in my greatest asset, which is my mind. Without financial literacy and discipline, I will achieve none of my goals. My real estate investments and other investments should be something of sound value I believe I can resell for a profit at a later date. After I have brought a property up to my own standards, I will sell it for a profit and buy another one to continue this process until I have acquired the money I desire.

Orientation: Introducing the Success and Wealth Equation!

The entrepreneur's path is a dirt road that has been washed out often by the rains of failure. Getting stuck in the muck is expected and will bring forth a separation of characters. Losers call a tow truck and never return to the path, in fear of getting stuck again. Winners go out and purchase a winch.

—J. L. Williams

Here it is—the crème de la crème of all success and financial books. It took me writing this book to find and shape it into a coherent formula. You won't find it in your high school or college textbooks. I could take my time explaining how you need to align yourself with the universe and all that other new age crap, but I won't bother. My time and yours is of the upmost importance and I'm not going to sell you "feel-good" beliefs. If you want those, then scan the horoscopes or "Dear Abby" column of your local paper.

While those "feel-good" and "positive" belief systems are important to success, they are only half the equation which can only lead to half-assed results (go figure). I want you to feel rich on the inside as well as become rich on the outside.

I cannot say or tell you what being rich means to *you*. It is your job to search out that answer for yourself. That's why, at this time, it is also imperative to find out what amount of money you need to supplement your lifestyle, goals, and intentions. Remember, make it as definite as possible and set a specific date for its acquisition. Yes, this is really a workbook and you will *need* to participate in order to see any results.

Ok, now that you have figured up that amount of money, go ahead and write it down right here on this page. Or on every page if you feel like it. Highlight it, circle it, underline it, whatever. This is your money goal. Get familiar with it. Think, dream, and act on it regularly. Interaction is required. Developing your passion for it is expected. Grab your bank statement and write down the amount you want to see there by the date you have chosen. Tack this to your collage so you can see it everyday.

It is my job to give you a swift kick in the ass and point you in the right direction, but understand that I cannot make the journey for you. No one is going to hold your hand or sing old Tears for Fears songs to you when you're feeling down and out. You have to pull your own weight and scale the mountain that is blocking your view and path to the Forest of Prosperity.

Here's the equation that has worked for me and continues to reign supreme as a basic plan and schematic for acquiring success in today's times. I'm throwing you a rope. Climb up and let's witness the distant horizon for a moment.

30% Possessing the desire and ability to break society's widely misconstrued view of wealth and success. Conditioning yourself to accept and believe that you are worthy of becoming a successful and independent person and can think outside the limitations of a job.

30% Figuring out which routes to money you will travel. Which is the quickest and most fit for your set of skills? The building, testing, and crafting of these theories into something that works, preferably without giving thirty of your truest "golden years" away.

40% Protection that only comes from the experience and discipline you've gained and set in place to guard your lifestyle from vain and superficial images/desires. Also the fine tuning and organization of your most powerful and stimulating desires/emotions: sex, love, power, faith, and gratitude. These will feed and sustain the goldfish pond in that bright and dreamy head of yours.

Prerequisite: Literacy Skills—Feeding the Goldfish with Words and Ideas

Read books by people who have accomplished what you want to achieve. Model their behaviors and actions and thoughts—try to imagine what they must have thought when they walked along the path you are now treading. They are every bit as human as we are so that means that we can achieve whatever they achieved, if we can model their formulas for success—their thoughts, behaviors, and actions.

Here you might say, "But, I don't like reading." Then buy an audio book. A fascinating concept really. All you need are your ears and a competent mind. YouTube is full of them. It sure beats the hell out of watching music artists talk about their diamond grillz or millions stacked in the bank while they cruise around in two hundred thousand dollar cars, unless of course you aspire to be a rapper driving an exotic car while talking about the same crap in every song.

How many songs can you write about blunts and bitches? Apparently a lot. It could be a prosperous career for you. Look at Jay-Z or P. Diddy. Their music careers funded the creation of other streams of income. They are now multi-millionaire rappers. I'm sure you won't be surprised to learn that Master P was on the *Forbes* list of highest-paid entertainers in 1998.

What made the difference for these rappers is that they shifted their thoughts from those of consumers (buyers) to those of producers (sellers). Each of them has (or has had) his own clothing line and record company. They are producers now, where the big money is to be made. Sell fifty million albums or fifty million T-shirts and guess what? You stand to make a lot of those Benjamins you hear about in the songs.

The World Needs More Dream Enablers

More of your time should be spent investing in something that can better your future, right? Otherwise what's the point of living? Stop worrying and start living.

If you have a complaint, then devote ten minutes of your time to writing down solutions for this problem or stall point. Within some of those pesky problems are million-dollar solutions if you can find the complementary underlying problem and solve it, over and over again until you're a millionaire. Repeat formula. Become a multi-millionaire. You get the idea.

Worry less about keeping up with the Joneses and focus on *your* dreams and ambitions. Stoke the flame of your desire. Feed your inner drive and awaken the person inside who has wanted to burst out of your cage for a while. Yeah! That feels good, doesn't it? It seems as though your breathing has been restored and you can inhale deeply of that sweet oxygen around you.

Maybe your dream or goal—or can we call it dream goal? Works for me. Maybe your dream goal is to go horseback riding. You imagine yourself galloping along on your beautiful black stallion or mustang, maybe in an open field or somewhere far off in the desert. Or perhaps your dream is running in a marathon through the streets of downtown New Orleans, listening to U2's *Where the Streets Have No Name* on your iPod. Only you know what *you* truly want out of this circus wheel we call life.

Think about your deepest desire for a moment. See if you can search out the source of the fire burning beneath it and feed it an influential accelerant. This starts with cultivating your imagination.

Who is in the driver's seat of your life? Answer in short detail: *you*. You are the ultimate factor in the equation. Can you see yourself in that new position and feel the benefits of becoming that new you? If you can, then you are well on your way to new ideas and fresh thoughts. Let them into your mind and oppose all negative opposition. You can still be polite when stepping apart from the status quo. Then again, maybe you are in favor of certain aspects of the status quo.

If you do not see great riches in your imagination, you will never see them in your bank balance.

—Napoleon Hill

Logic and Responsible Self-Talk

No! I'm not crazy. Those people talk to therapists, not themselves!

I took an entry level class in college called finite mathematics and when I wasn't busy daydreaming about the hot brunette two rows over, I learned that a basic understanding of logic and reasoning lies at the heart of vocabulary.

If seeing is believing, then the inverse holds true as well. Believing is seeing. What the mind imagines and what it manifests derive from the same source. They are one in the same, intermingled and fused together, and your mind cannot tell the difference. Here's a great example of logic from *Alice's Adventures in Wonderland*.

If I had a world of my own, everything would be nonsense. Nothing would be what it is, because everything would be what it isn't. And contrary wise, what is, it wouldn't be. And what it wouldn't be, it would. You see?

—Lewis Carroll

Here is where self-talk and the advancement of your vocabulary become remarkably important, not only to make you sound like you have more than a sixth grade education when speaking to others, but also for the benefit of sending intelligent commands to the most sophisticated computer ever: your brain.

Do you use these words—all, none, some, many? How about these: abundance, zilch, a portion, multiple? Or the pimps of Vocabulary Avenue: opulent progression, superfluous nihility, multitudinous showers of affluence, perpetual latitudes and fathoms of immense prosperity?

The daily self-talk and dialogue running at all times of the day in your head can be edited and revised to fit your objectives and dreams. Instead of stating shaky and doubtful premises such as: *I don't know if we will ever climb out from under this pile of debt!* Say this: *I will climb out from under this pile of debt because I let the situation get out of control, but I do now hereby commit to focusing on creating more income to pay back the creditors in a timely fashion.* No doubt can come by way of that statement. Responsibility stepped in and smashed it lifeless.

Internal Psychology Creates External Reality

Here are some preconceived notions about the greenbacks in your pocket, provided you actually have a few dollars to your name. Listen up and heed the call! Have you adopted any of these maxims for your internal dialogue?

⇨ Money is hard to come by. (I'm not buying this grotesque idea and neither should you. It makes me want to hurl at the thought of this statement actually taking form in my book!)

⇨ My job doesn't pay a lot of money. (How much did you ask for? Have you set up any *passive* income streams to supplement your cash flow?)

⇨ The love of money is the root of all evil. (The latter part of that Bible verse commonly left out and much needed for clarification—which while some coveted after. Don't believe me? Look it up for yourself: 1 Timothy 6:10 (KJV). Notice the keyword being *some*)

⇨ Money comes from an infinite source. (The original source being your mind's capacity and desire to collect, organize, and intelligently apply your ideas to the real world, and I do mean "real world".)

⇨ It takes money to make money. (Yes, it's easier to make money when you have it stockpiled and know how to leverage your resources. Do you want to know what it really takes to make money? Money can flow easier to you when you possess something of value that you can sell to interested parties.)

⇨ Money buys the freedom to think, do, and act as I please. (No you can't avoid paying taxes. Not unless you want to go to prison for tax evasion.)

The last statement does not entail that you are somehow above the supreme laws of our universe. In this life, you will ultimately reap what you sow. Get used to it. Find better seeds to plant and you have a good probability of success for next year's crop. Aerate the soil and fertilize annually—even higher probability of success. Install irrigation systems, let Mother Nature do her job, give thanks and share gratitude for the blessings of the previous year's crops—then you have formulated a working plan for success.

Conditioning 102—Emotional Stimulants and Frugality

Love can be a very powerful catalyst for pushing your motivation levels into the exosphere. We all crave it and the emotional attachments that make our lives blossom and radiate with full abundance of life. This takes up a substantial amount of our everyday lives. Take that love you have for something, harness it, and realize its potential. It's wonderful, isn't it?

You are sole owner of it and decide how to allocate your love currency. You might give up a portion for a girlfriend, spouse, lover, roommate, next-door neighbor, family pet, etc. I personally prefer to differentiate my streams of love and direct them at will, much like a crane operator offloads a ship. I can move it here and there to my liking and tolerance.

Answer this: If someone or something you love was pushing/motivating you to be the absolute best, how much quicker do you think you'll achieve your goals and objectives? Think of a fire. You strike the match or flick your Bic and, voilà, the fire is born. It then spreads to any and all flammable materials around it (friends and family that believe in your talents) and lives on, fueled by the oxygen in the atmosphere. All of that transpires because *you* lit the flame.

To live rich really means acquiring a wealthy state of mind. There is nothing wrong with being frugal, but don't let that be the main focus behind your wealth creation. If it is, count on slow accumulation. Being thrifty will help you save money but will not explode your income—major bummer!

If friends and neighbors around you are content living frugally, then let them be. Don't worry about them. *You* like I stated earlier, are the ultimate factor in the equation. Look out for number one at all times.

Take a minute and think about *you*. I know it's selfish and all that jazz, possibly even naïve, but this shit is important so take it seriously. You should be so thoroughly consumed by who you want to be that you will ultimately become that which you think the most. Damn, that almost sounded philosophical!

Is your foot on the accelerator or is your vehicle (body) in park? Do you want to step on the fricking gas and never look back? Stop worrying about what other people are doing. And certainly stop talking about it. At the end of the day, right before you crawl under the sheets, realize that the only thing which you have control over is yourself.

SEX! SEX! SEX!

I thought if I had a chapter about sex, then everyone who saw the contents would jump right to it. Ooooooh, that's sounds interesting. Let me see what he says about that. If you want to sell a product in this country, sex is a highly effective motivator. The Hardee's restaurant chain even pulled it off with a cheeseburger commercial.

Sex is our most primal and innate desire, spreading its tentacles over the minds of women and men and allowing them to achieve great feats and possibilities. This desire will build up over time and wants to release its energy somewhere (copulation, masturbation, or maybe in creative ways such as painting or playing music).

A healthy sex life is part of a happy life. Wouldn't you agree with that? Pleasure is good. It's freaking fantastic to tell you the truth. Greek philosopher Epicurus said to avoid pleasure when pain follows—more golden advice picked up from my college western civilization class. Those are words of wisdom worth reading over again.

You can direct the energy from your sexual desires, just like my crane offloading the shipping containers at the dock, to your dreams and goals. I'm not talking about perverting or desecrating your life or image. I'm talking about harnessing the desire and making it work for you, letting the energy flow through your dream, giving it fuel for its ascension and acquirement.

Cultivate your emotions of sex, love, power, faith, and gratitude. Nurture them because they are the finely tuned traits contributing to your "becoming." Your spirit will cry out to be freed until the mind and body listen and begin to contribute to the situation.

Free Education—It's Everywhere!

Find some authors who have written books about achieving what you would like to achieve. C'mon, how much does it cost to check out books from the library? The last time I checked, it was a public service, paid for by your tax dollars. If you are paying for something, you might as well use it to your advantage.

In modern libraries, you can rent movies for about a dollar, and borrow audio books, games, hardcover books, paperbacks, fiction, non-fiction, and even check your e-mail or read *The Times* or *Rolling Stone Magazine*. Whatever you seek can usually be found inside the ultimate hub of information and knowledge.

Employ your time in improving yourself by other men's writings, so that you shall gain easily what others have labored hard for.
—Socrates

A Word on Seminars

I've attended about three different house flipping seminars held by some of the biggest names in the business. They're the ones doing the radio commercials and hiring public speakers to give FREE presentations in cities with "hot real estate markets."

If my memory serves correctly, the first one promoted a three day course covering all their flipping secrets to the tune of $1600 dollars. I enjoyed the free gourmet turkey sandwich and Mountain Dew, and left with a few notes about investing in tax liens—a complimentary bonus presentation!

The second seminar I found myself at one of the prestigious hotels in the downtown district. Free CD-ROM and a few scribbles later, they want about $500 bucks for the same three day course. The third one, which I went to only a few months ago, had me fired up after hearing this guy's story and offer—about $197 dollars for, you guessed it, another three day course.

When I made it to the table with my credit card, I froze for about ten to fifteen seconds, unable to understand why I needed to give anyone two hundred dollars for an education I could pick up from a twenty dollar book. Libraries would put the price at virtually nothing and lend me the same information, without such hefty price tags!

Words Are Weak Unless Backed by Persistent Action

When setting goals, there should always be a challenge to its acquisition, not easily achieved (slacker!). Growth is the sustainer of life. There is nothing you cannot accomplish if you choose to *act* upon your beliefs and follow through with persistence, will, and determination. Faith will move with you as well, brightening your eyes so that you may see clearly and have a better understanding of yourself.

Always be thankful for what you do have with full intention to keep striving for better things. Guide your attention with love and passion, direction, and dedication so you will accomplish whatever goal you set by the date you set for its achievement. Life will carry you away and at its end, what will the people left behind have to say about you? "He was a rotten bastard!" (Hopefully not.)

Maybe you'll be remembered for buying groceries for someone who had fallen on hard times. Maybe you're the proud owner of a huge restaurant chain who gives out to the needy every year for the holidays. The sky is the limit here. What do *you* really want to do? This is your most apropos moment. You may feel it so deeply that you will step out on faith and do it, not only for yourself, but also to prove to others that it can be done so that they might be inspired to change their own lives.

Here's another important question to ask yourself. What could you achieve if you operated at full potential—mentally, emotionally, physically, and spiritually? We have been told we use only a miniscule amount of our brainpower, insinuating that we have not achieved our greatest potential as human beings.

You must aspire to be more than a bum who watches *Matlock* reruns all day or jives away time killing zombies on Xbox LIVE. Is that your purpose on this sumptuous earth? Certainly don't want to cast a negative light on either one of these two activities.

They are both excellent pastimes but shouldn't be regarded as full-time endeavors. Don't dwell on pastimes too long unless you have twenty-five million dollars in the bank and can afford whatever pastime you desire. We live in the present tense for good reason.

>FOCUS: FIRST AND FOREMOST<

Keep your eyes on the ultimate prize at all times. Put your focus and energy into what you want, not what you don't want. Imagine yourself already in possession of what you most desire. That hot rod (your profitable ideas) wants to escape the garage and show the world its true potential and talents. If you can display confidence in yourself and your work, then you can produce loyal customers. These are the people whose money you'll accept and deposit in your bank account in exchange for products or services.

Ask any employee in Wal-Mart what the number one rule of customer service is. I'll bet the answer will be, "The customer is always right." Why do you think that is? Happenstance maybe? Try no. Successful business owners realize that if they can please their customers in every way possible, then their customers will continue to spend money there. People like folks who take pride in their work and have totally immersed themselves in their craft and passion.

The consumer likes reliability, prompt service, and honesty. Provide all three and you hit the jackpot. Money flows more easily into your life if you can fill a need as quickly and efficiently as possible. This will take hard work and possibly years of sacrifice and dedication. Are you up for this so-called daunting task or would you rather struggle for the rest of your life? I don't think the job market will suddenly disappear, so you can begin crafting your idea part-time. No excuses, remember?

If you can do anything extraordinarily well, then you have a marketable idea and a way of providing revenue for your household. All it takes is one simple idea—one that can grow in your imagination like a forest fire in a high wind.

Every human being who reaches the age of understanding of the purpose of money, wishes for it. Wishing will not bring riches. But desiring riches with a state of mind that becomes an obsession, then planning definite ways and means to acquire riches, and backing those plans with persistence which does not recognize failure will bring riches.

—Napoleon Hill

Figuring 101—Lesson in Consumer Demand

There are more than enough goods, products, and services that American consumers (actually, most of the developed world) will continue to want and need throughout the course of their lives. Examine your skill set and knowledge as they relate to each category, if applicable. Which areas are the strongest for you?

⇨ Communication (cell phone, fax, internet, good old fashioned mail)

⇨ Transportation (bicycle, vehicle, bus, subway, airfare)

⇨ Fuel (hydrogen, oil, gasoline, diesel, ethanol)

⇨ Insurance (vehicle, house, renter's, life, health)

⇨ Shelter (lease, mortgage, rent)

⇨ Clothing (shoes, hats, jeans, t-shirts, belts, purses)

⇨ Consumer Staples (food, beverages, household items, tobacco)

⇨ Utilities (electricity, water, natural gas, sewer, garbage or recycling service)

⇨ Information and knowledge (colleges and universities, trade schools, magazines, e-books, seminars, blogs, forums)

⇨ Entertainment (radio, television, music albums, movies, novels, art, leisure)

⇨ Personal services (This list is growing daily. Consulting, cleaning, monogramming, painting, plumbing, construction, demolition, moving, babysitting, pet sitting, accounting and legal, electronics repair, glass repair, nutrition and fitness, writing, organizing, beauty, reading, web design, financial, advertising, photography, coaching, and music lessons.)

These are just a few off the top of my head. I'm sure some people's lists would far exceed this one. Channel locks, cable, laundry detergent, coffee, bleach, toilet plungers, paperclips, deodorant—should you choose to wear it.

Every one of those things is likely in your home right now, bought and paid for by the consumer spirit within you. In order to acquire wealth, you must switch your thinking over from that of a consumer to that of a *producer* or plainly stated—become a person who creates economic value with your salable goods and services.

Let's say I gave you one hundred unlabeled bottles of water which you could sell for whatever price you desire. Would you sell them without labels or try your luck at creating a catchy label to grab buyer interest and put more money in your pocket?

What would make your product or service better than the rest? After all, it's just spring water. Ultimately, this book was just an assortment of words until it was assimilated and organized into a user friendly manual for personal finance and success.

Think about personal finance books for a moment. Many titles on the best-sellers list contain the same old crap we've been consuming for decades—go to college and get a degree, find a good job, avoid credit card debt, pour money into your 401(k) plan, take the time to cut coupons, spend the next thirty years paying off a mortgage, attain a spot in heaven, spoil your grandkids, etc. Why do you think I wrote this book? The idea grew from my complaint of—*I'm tired of reading this crap. Can somebody please share a new perspective on this subject?* Damn right somebody can.

Wallace D. Wattles published his book *The Science of Getting Rich* in 1910 and before him was James Allen with *As a Man Thinketh*, out in 1902. Napoleon Hill published *The Law of Success* in 1928. Yes, information about achieving more than a job with great benefits has been out there for a long time. Why don't the school systems believe these books are relevant and applicable to "real world" success? Don't have a clue.

Things that have been rethought and reorganized so they appear new always come along. Mobile home gives way to brick house, Kobe follows in Jordan's footsteps, Blu-ray disc player annihilates VHS tapes, MP3 sales slaughter those of compact discs. You see where I'm going with this?

The world as we have created it is a process of our thinking. It cannot be changed without changing our thinking.
—Albert Einstein

Building and Testing 101—Brand Recognition and Loyalty

Let's talk about one of the bestselling products ever—the iPhone. If you own one or ever have, I bet you loved it, didn't you? Ok, maybe I'm talking to myself here mostly. The iPhone and smartphone markets gave rise to several other subsectors:

⇨ Digital media (music, e-books, apps)

⇨ Protective cases, screen protectors

⇨ Chargers, docking stations

⇨ Headphones, beatbox

As you see, one product spawned multiple other business ideas. This list could easily apply to the growing tablet market as well. I've even seen new businesses in my area that will cater to those clumsy folks who always seem to drop and crack their cell phone screens. There's a $99 dollar repair waiting to happen. Trust me, I found myself at one of these places not long after my LCD screen found the wrong side of a billiard table.

Plant an apple seed and along comes a young sapling after careful planning and nourishment. At first, it's puny and needs reinforcement, but after annual pruning and fertilization, it grows thick with age and you soon discover flowers starting to bloom. It isn't long before the branches become heavy with the weight of fifty to a hundred apples, each with enough seeds to plant an entire garden.

Maybe you could create the next generation of iPhone cases made entirely out of alligator skin and sell them for eight hundred dollars apiece on the Internet. Get this though; your case design is submersible much like the LifeProof® cases. I know, gnarly idea right? Sell a thousand and guess how much you'd gross? Eight hundred thousand dollars.

Not really. That's just a simple mathematical formula without real world variables. There would be other associated costs—the cost of manufacturing, shipping, possibly employee salaries, website-related expenses, taxes, and the hours you spend investing your precious time in this idea.

Problems might pop into your head: you don't have any 'gator skin, the economy sucks right now, you have a headache, your waiting on your income tax check to come back, blah, blah, blah. Stop with the excuses. I don't want to hear them and neither does anyone else. Go ahead and ask yourself: Do you have problems or do you have solutions?

Creative Crafting 101—Alchemize Your Ideas Using Your Passion

Maybe you're a devout health nut who has put together an awesome cookbook for healthy living after you notice your friends and family always asking for recipes concerning healthy diet choices. You are able to sell fifteen thousand copies through Amazon's distribution system after only a year of implementing and refining your marketing strategy. Social media websites (Facebook, Twitter, Google+, Pinterest) are making it easier to build your business name or promote your product.

The idea here is to stimulate you to think of helping the consumer, not just playing the part of consumer. Find a way to help people solve their problems and offer a specific service or product. If you're passionate about doing this something, then half the war is already won. It could be something simple like dog sitting for your friends when they are on vacation. Will that fifty dollars make you rich? Obviously not, but this may spawn a side venture like a dog sitting business.

There are people out there—excuse me, there are *customers* out there, your prospects, who would enjoy paying you because you have such an awesome product or service that benefits them and provides top-notch value in their lives.

Larry's Lawn Care: Fishing Locally

I meet folks all the time who think they have discovered a gold nugget of knowledge: "Yeah I know but there are so many people doing that right now." Who cares? Do it better. Stand out in the crowd. Don't give up because Larry's Lawn Care has three commercial lawnmowers and you have only one. In fact, you could probably learn an important lesson from Larry. He has opted to invest back into his business and now has six full-time employees and three trucks that run sixty or more hours a week.

Larry has discovered something truly magical. He invested a portion of his earnings and, from that seed, the company expanded and now earns three times as much as it did when he had just his truck and himself doing the work. You are every bit as smart as Larry and, while you can't exactly be Larry (he's my character—get your own!) you can certainly learn to model his behaviors, thus providing you with Larry-like results: more of those greenbacks in your pocket.

Larry understands the advantage of leveraging his time and resources. He has taken on several new employees and now spends his days talking to customers and bidding on jobs. He's also established a foreman on his crew to oversee the employees and pays him a tidy forty thousand dollar salary. The foreman thinks this is a pay raise from his last *J-O-B* but Larry is thinking about how his business has grown to achieve a four-hundred-thousand-dollar revenue stream and the contracts get bigger every year as his manpower grows and improves.

Notice the monetary difference in thinking. This is the shift from employee to business owner. If you are going to be rich, and I'm talking about a million or more in net worth, then you will need a formula for wealth—one in which you can leverage simple mathematics in your favor. This is a vital tool for success.

Planning a Deep Sea Fishing Voyage

To What Extent Do You Want To Make a Difference?

Let's say you wrote an e-book about something you know how to do well. Then you sold your product online through ebooks.com, Amazon, or other distribution channels (your website). By this time next year, you've sold around forty thousand copies at $7 profit (royalty payment). That's a quarter-million dollar idea, with change left over! Ballin!

This idea is once again without real world representation. First, you would need to have created a product that is desirable and marketable to a wide audience. Books take time to write and market, meanwhile you just put in a really long and stressful day at work. Never mind you have to pay the rent or mortgage this week. Where will you find the time for business ideas?

> *If you really want to do something, you'll find a way. If you don't, you'll find an excuse.*
>
> —Jim Rohn

I don't expect everyone who reads this wants to be a writer. I'm just showing you the simple formula needed to acquire a stream of passive income and potentially big money. I don't know, maybe you want to sell coffee beans or flip-flops to the world (I recently read a story about a 15 year old *entrepreneur* that was persistent enough and now sells her colorful flip-flops to huge retailers, such as Macy's and Nordstrom! She has already generated over a million dollars in income at fifteen years of age—this girl rocks!) Your passion is all your own. The formula stays the same, only the variables change. Still want a job with annual 3% pay raises for thirty years?

Riches come fast and in abundance to the person who understands how to fill a need on a much larger scale. Let's say for example that you mow lawns in your local demographic—a forty-five mile radius. There is a select number of people in that location—I'll take a random guess and say a possible one to thirty million. In my area, there's just over a million people within a sixty mile radius. This number is entirely dependent upon your given location.

We are fishing in a freaking pond here! The odds of reeling in a black-fin tuna in these waters are slim to none. There will be several small prizes awarded to the person fishing in the pond—brim, bass, or catfish. One to two meals, tops, is what you'll get, not a freezer full of meat (residual income) to last you all season.

At this point our pal Larry decides he wants to grow even further with his lawn-care business but isn't sure how, given his forty-five mile radius approach. It's time for creative thinking or, in layman's terms, it is time to put that thinking cap on!

If I were having a conversation with Larry, I would ask him what other things he or his crew can do well. He says he's been interested in installing irrigation systems for upscale neighborhoods ever since he saw crews at work in his own neighborhood.

He wants to update his computer software for pipe layout and integrated timers. This isn't something he's tried before so he's apprehensive. Yes, it's uncharted waters and it will be a bit deeper than the pond, but that's why there is discovery. If you don't try it, you'll never know what might have happened, and who really wants to live with that turmoil?

Am I saying you need to start a landscaping company to get rich? Absolutely not, though I am sure there are landscaping business owners who do very well for themselves. I want you to see the basic idea behind this fictitious story—success in any undertaking takes a high level of creativity and being able to adapt to the persistent winds of change. Make sure you are strapped in for the long haul because it can be a bumpy ride!

Get Rich! Super Quick and Easy! Buy a Ticket *Today*!

I would say the quickest way to get rich is to play the lotto. Ha! Ha! I sincerely hope you don't believe that crock of shit. If you happened to win the lottery, would you really be capable of knowing what to do with the money in order to preserve it? Could you make it last the rest of your life? It's doubtful, because you skipped the essential process of earning the money, therefore missing out on the lessons that allowed you to keep that amount of money safely protected from selfish desires and superficial images.

Provide a service (creation), get the word out (marketing), and sell (distribution) yourself and your product. Maybe you provide prerecorded guitar lessons via the website you created, like a professional guitar player friend of mine is working on. With the Internet, you can provide your product or service to almost any country in the world—although mowing someone's grass in Saudi Arabia is obviously an implausible idea. Now *that* is an ocean of fish.

Maybe you create an exclusive jewelry line for women that really takes off after a few years, and you sell a million dollars' worth of merchandise in a single month. Anything is possible here. Offer people something they want badly or demand highly, and you can become rich quickly. Basic arithmetic.

If you have ever used eBay to sell a product, then you have the basic platform and setup for acquiring wealth in this country. I'm not saying you need an eBay account to strike it rich, but I am suggesting that you start one to understand the scope of selling goods and products to consumers in the world. Experience teaches more than reading any book on finance or success.

People grow through experience if they meet life honestly and courageously. This is how character is built.

—Eleanor Roosevelt

The important thing to remember is to never let go of those hopes and dreams. Think back to when you were a child and the world was one big, mysterious place. You felt like anything was possible because you knew no better. You saw no boundaries or limitations.

What you did know was that you wanted certain things and that you were meant to have them, even if it meant begging Mom and Dad for an entire year to get it. That desire burned inside you until you thought it would pierce your skin. Cultivate that childish imagination again. Crank those rusty gears in your brain and the blinds of adulthood can fall off.

Why Am I Broke All the Time?

If I were broke, this is the question I would ask myself—but I'm not and never will be again. I made up my mind to do whatever I needed to do early in life to be ahead financially when I'm older. Hopefully you don't have to ask yourself this embarrassing and demeaning question. Hopefully you have not accepted this sob story as your life.

You and I see people every day who are comfortable with being broke, as though it were a natural part of life. The idea here is to live abundantly, not in poverty and wondering how your water pump will get fixed so you can make it to your dead-end job on Monday.

Every man also to whom God hath given riches and wealth, and hath given him power to eat thereof, and to take his portion, and to rejoice in his labour; this is the gift of God.
—Ecclesiastes 5: 19 (KJV)

There is plenty on this earth to go around several times over. To accept any less than that would be treasonous to your thinking and actions. Know that you do not have to accept a mediocre life with its endless, mundane realities and routines. Strive for better things and better circumstances. Better life and better health. Better family relationships and friendships. You are the creator and sculptor of your life. God won't condemn you to the fiery depths of hell if you make a few mistakes along the way.

A life lived in fear of making mistakes is a sheltered one with little growth and discovery. Don't limit your abilities. Be open-minded and dream big. Try new ways of doing things. Be yourself, do good deeds, and provide value to other people.

If you can do that and keep the right mental attitude, then I believe God will move obstacles aside for you, as long as your efforts are pure and altruistic in nature. Remember the golden rule? Do unto others as you would have them do unto you? How could you possibly go wrong living by that example? It is completely pure in thought.

An Ultimatum for Job Seekers and Over Spenders

If money is what you want, then make a stake for it and stand your ground. Whatever amount you set out to earn is rightfully yours, but no one is saying the trip will be easy. If you want easy, go find a job.

The problem with that is the mentality and approach of many job seekers today—"I need to find a good paying job with benefits". That puts more focus on you, the employee and less the customer (your lifeline). Think how and where can I provide the most value for people today? Which areas suit me the best? Where could my skills blossom the most?

Jobs are great building blocks for success and can possibly unfold a career change into self-employment. Switching over to producer again. Now you can be the one to help create and provide jobs in your community. This is fifth gear or what is commonly known as overdrive and you will work harder on your product or business and put in more hours than you ever did at your day job, at least during the primitive stages of development. Visualize, plan, execute, and listen to the feedback. Adjust and repeat the formula.

A logical reason why you might be broke is because you don't manage your money well. Make five hundred dollars a week, spend half of it buying shots for your drunken friends and buddies on the weekend. Hello to a broke and destitute Monday morning.

This is a lifestyle that will leave your pockets empty if you don't get it under control. Purchase an enjoyable bottle of single-barrel whiskey or wine and eat the most expensive steak (eggplant for you vegans) for dinner, and you can still come out ahead. Going broke does not equal happiness.

In other words, your lifestyle must match your earnings. Need I say anymore? If you want to drive a Porsche to work every day, then go buy one. You can finance it. Sixty thousand dollars of debt? Hey, no problem! But if you plan to take on this kind of debt, I sincerely hope you are making more annually than the cost of the car coming off the lot. Do you want to look like a winner, or actually be a winner? It's fun to be flashy and extravagant at times, but don't be consumed by it.

I've read that Warren Buffett, the legendary billionaire investor, still lives in the same home he bought in 1957 for $31,500. Think about the return on his investment. He has continued to improve the property over the years, making his return compound in value.

How Much Money Are You Saving?

This is equally important to your goals and pertinent to becoming a financially responsible adult. You should save at least 10 percent of your earnings and find ways to save more. Think of side projects or other endeavors that can pay you on a consistent basis.

Think multiple streams of income. Money from your job, loose change collection—laugh but you have to start somewhere—interest on your bank balance, stock dividends and gains, liquidation of your real estate and/or rent from tenants, eBay account, passive income from website, royalties from copyrighted material such as videos, books, or music albums.

The habit of saving money requires more force of character than most people have developed, for the reason that saving means self-denial and sacrifice of amusements and pleasures in scores of different ways.

—Napoleon Hill, *The Law of Success*

According to a survey performed by 24/7 Wall St., Ireland ranks as the country that saves the most money, with residents putting aside an average of 19.3 percent of their income in savings. Maybe this is where the luck of the Irish comes from? Average Americans save around 5.8 percent of their incomes. This is not good enough to get ahead in these debt-laden times.

As a country, we have become lazy and complacent about where we are and who we are. Many people have become content and OK with their current status or station in life. They do nothing about their problems but complain to anyone who will listen to their self-inflicted victim portrayal. I guess that's easier than taking any real action.

You will never become financially independent until *you* take charge and accept responsibility for your life and financial well-being. If you enjoy luxuries, then you will need money in the bank to achieve that four-week vacation in Bora Bora or that cruise to Cozumel. Nothing is free.

There is always a price to pay and sacrifices to make on your end of the bargain. To be wealthy (the minority, around 1% of the population) in your life, you will have to think and act unlike the majority of people. This simple logic is a gold mine if understood.

Financial Foundationing 101

Every well-built house needs a solid foundation on which to stand. The financial groundwork you lay should complement your dreams and goals. Put money aside as often as possible. Set up a spare-change jar or container in your bedroom. Call up your bank or financial institution—relationships with banks are important for certain goals you might want to achieve—and see what kind of dividend you earn on your money.

The truth is that nowadays, most banks (suck) don't offer a decent return on your money. I called my former bank one day to ask what percentage I was earning on my money. Take a wild guess. The rate was a whopping 0.03 percent, aka three-hundredths of a cent on every dollar I had invested in the bank. At the time I had over twenty thousand dollars in that account and earned around ten cents in interest every month. At that rate, I could buy a stick of chewing gum in about three months time—what a joke!

Bank Alternatives: Credit Unions and Online Banks

Credit unions are member owned organizations, not corporately owned like the big banks that are traded publically on Wall Street. I found one in my area that offered a high yield checking account with a 2.5 percent interest rate (this is a *higher* yield than most other establishments).

Look, it's quite obvious you won't get rich with interest income but with enough capital you can create passive cash flow into your life. They may be small gains at first and celebrating them may seem trivial to some, but if you get excited about the small wins, it will open up your mind to see the possibility of the larger picture at stake.

Credit unions usually want you to do a few things, such as making twelve to fifteen debit purchases, signing up for e-statements, etc., before you can earn that special interest rate, but it is minimal work. Other alternatives to traditional savings may include: money market accounts, CDs (certificate of deposit), or internet banks that can provide higher interest rates than local brick and mortar establishments. Check out: www. Bankrate.com for ways to compare options.

Automated Savings

Set up an automatic debit of ten percent of your paycheck to move from checking to savings every payday. If you say you can't afford that, then you should ask yourself why you're reading this book. Look down at your feet and ask yourself how much those shoes set you back.

Saving money becomes habit forming and then guess what happens? Down the road, when you get a raise or promotion or a side job—leveraging your job skills outside of your employment for quick cash—you'll decide to up your original investment of ten percent to fifteen percent a week. This is my dummied up version of a personal 401(k) fund—none of those pesky restraints or limitations and not a money manager in sight, except for you. (In 2013, the maximum contribution you can make to your employer's 401(k) plan is $17,500. Does anyone think that you can get rich when someone (the IRS) is limiting how much you can contribute to this "safe" investment?)

From that seedling you can invest in mutual funds, exchange-traded funds (ETFs), stocks, real estate, commodities, bonds, options and futures contracts, and other routes to grow your money even further. It's a fascinating world out there if you open your eyes and look around. Can you lose money in these other financial instruments I have mentioned? Yes, you certainly can, so I advise you to thoroughly know the ins and outs of the market you desire to enter.

Carpe Diem and a FREE Resource List!

I like to ask myself what I can do without today to bring me a nicer tomorrow. All those old compact discs—who the hell needs 'em? It's all MP3 now anyway. Time to start liquidating on eBay. Got a leaf blower sitting idle in your garage? Maybe you happened to hear a friend complaining about his front porch and driveway being covered in leaves. There's a quick fifty dollars in your savings. Or maybe you enjoy refinishing antique furniture and can strike a deal with a local distributor.

There is something that *you* can do better than most others who try. It comes naturally to you, like you were ordained for it. Find out what that is and invest your precious time there whole-heartedly. You might find Malcolm Gladwell's book *Outliers* intriguing. His chapter on the ten-thousand-hour rule is enlightening and there is much you can absorb from the entire book.

Here are some of the books I have read over the years and found some piece of truth—or even humor—within:

⇨ Napoleon Hill—*Think and Grow Rich*

⇨ M. J. DeMarco—*The Millionaire Fastlane*

⇨ Anthony Robbins—*Unlimited Power*

⇨ T. Harv Eker—*Secrets of the Millionaire Mind*

⇨ Denis Waitley—*The Psychology of Winning*

⇨ Alan Corey—*A Million Bucks by 30*

⇨ Peter Lynch, John Rothchild—*One Up on Wall Street*

⇨ Michael Corbett—*Find It, Fix It, Flip It!: Make Millions in Real Estate—One House at a Time*

⇨ Nicolas Darvas—*How I Made $2,000,000 in the Stock Market*

⇨ Jason Kelly—*Financially Stupid People Are Everywhere: Don't Be One Of Them*

⇨ Jason Kelly—*The Neatest Little Guide to Stock Market Investing*

⇨ Jack D. Schwager—*Market Wizards: Interviews With Top Traders*

These books have brought me great inspiration, new thought, and, in the cases of Corey's book, laughter in heaping piles. Maybe they will help you in some way as they did for me when I was looking for inspiring people to model or just looking for a laugh. The library is full of books, but not necessarily full of great writers, so be careful what you read and who you believe. The truth is out there…enter *The X-Files* theme music.

III. THOUGHTS

ABOUT THE NEXT

TWENTY YEARS

And so, my fellow Americans: ask not what your country can do for you—ask what you can do for your country. My fellow citizens of the world: ask not what America will do for you, but what together we can do for the freedom of man.

—John F. Kennedy

The Distant Horizon From Your Perspective

I hope you have put some thought into the things I've discussed with you. Let me ask you another question. If you owned a DeLorean that could travel *Back to the Future*, would you change anything in your past to hopefully correct present-day circumstances, much as Marty did in the movie? More than likely there's something you would like to change.

If you examine the true bona fide winners, you'll see they have no need to show their wealth, for it shows in their every step and breath. Their prize is in the mastery of themselves. Provide the complementary attitude toward success. The more people you can reach out and help, the more you can reap the fruits of your actions.

Don't complain and gripe about your current situation in life. A year from now you won't even remember what you were fussing over. These problems are yours to solve for a specific reason. Who knows, you might just find a million-dollar idea in the midst of all your problems. If someone has a problem, you are the critical thinker who can solve their dilemma and happily save the day.

Maybe you would like to buy a bigger house in the next twenty years, preferably one with an upstairs and a hot tub. Something with brick and stucco this time, also a few more acres of land and horse stables for the equestrians out there. How will you afford these things without a sound and working financial plan?

Perhaps you'll invest in a new rental property every two years and, at the end of twenty years, will have collected ten properties that you collectively sell to another investor for $15 million. That is a realistic investment plan—not a supercharged route to wealth, but it will bring you there just the same.

Maybe you'll buy a house every two years and roll your equity and profits into a form 1031 like-kind exchange, which defers the taxation of capital gains. Many real estate investors use this approach, taking advantage of tax laws to grow their *net worth*. I am thinking of adapting this method myself.

When I sell a house or investment, I want to package it as a home. It's warm and inviting, and potential buyers' imaginations should take off when they see it. You need powerful catalysts to stir up human emotions when presenting your home to potential buyers. If you can create that emotional state, then you have sold an idea that can grow in the imagination. They can raise their kids here and live the American Dream. Woo-hoo!

You have once again shifted your thinking from consumer to producer. Your bank balance may not immediately reflect this, but you know that's OK because you are sowing money seedlings for your future, and you will harvest them in due time.

Keep working towards the amount of money you desire until you see it has manifested in your bank account (by your hard work and diligence of course). Remember Sir Issac Newton's first *law* of motion: An object at rest will remain at rest unless acted on by an unbalanced force. Provide that force and something will happen.

The purpose in your reading of other literature besides those sappy vampire-romance novels is to educate yourself so you may live more abundantly. I would confidently bet that the author of the *Twilight* series is not hurting for money after selling more than one hundred million copies worldwide. If you can sell one hundred million anything, then you will become insanely rich.

No one truly wants to live a poverty-stricken life, but several million people do every day in our free country, as if they deserve it or cannot escape its grasp on them. Do not fall into this trap and, better yet, don't hang around people who appear inundated with these problems.

Yes they need help, but only they can ask for it, and only they can muster the courage to change their lives. They will have to awaken themselves before anything good will come of them. You cannot force your ideas on a person and expect them to immediately stick. Emotions get all in the way.

Showing them the way is a much more appropriate approach to helping people with their issues.

If you want to help the poverty stricken, don't just say it. Donate food and volunteer your time to the area food bank in your neighborhood. They would be extremely grateful for a volunteer. Do good deeds and you will become rich in your own life.

What is your perception of being rich? House on the beach? Fancy super car? Or maybe just a happy family life and healthy children? Having more than enough to go around for everybody? Whatever it is, you can have it if you set your mind to receive it. Think about how you tune your radio to your favorite station. It has to be set at the exact frequency, otherwise you pick up nearby white noise and static.

IV. Larry's Take on Investing

One of the very nice things about investing in the stock market is that you learn about all different aspects of the economy. It's your window into a very large world.

—Ron Chernow

Larry Leverages the Stock Market

Our good buddy Larry has been saving money since he was eighteen years old. Every week after he made his paycheck, he put ten dollars from it into his savings account. After two years of not touching the funds, he had saved a little over one thousand dollars.

During his first year of college, he noticed a lot of students carrying around these slick-looking portable media devices. Technology giant Avucaudo produced and marketed the devices and they soon became a best-selling item worldwide. Everyone wanted one. Larry was browsing the Yahoo! website when he spotted the company traded on the NASDAQ under the ticker symbol GUAC for around thirty-two dollars a share.

He checked out a few books on investing from the library and found out how to create a brokerage account. He then funded his account with the money from his savings and bought as many shares of the company as he could.

Over the span of the next two years, the company excels and the value of the stock has almost tripled in value! Even better than that, Larry poured more money into the stock and now owns about one hundred shares. If and when he liquidates his position, he could pay up to fifteen percent on his long-term capital gains, depending on his income tax rate.

Only when the stock is sold does the capital gain or loss become realized. He's learned from his investing literature that taxation for long-term capital gains (*assets* held longer than a year) is significantly lower than the short-term (held for under a year) capital gains, which is taxed at ordinary income levels (ten to 39.6 percent).

All the while, Larry's daytime job provided a few pay increases and, being the kind of guy who takes initiative in his financial matters, he stepped up the original ten dollars a week savings to twenty-five dollars. Larry is living out his dreams—or at least working toward them.

He recognizes trends and invests his hard-earned capital in the companies involved—not necessarily in their products. He realizes goods and products can depreciate faster than stock values. His investments and brokerage account grow beyond the limitations of his bank account until, around his twenty-fifth birthday, his total account value now exceeds one hundred thousand dollars.

Reality Check

If we all started out as early as Larry did, we would have a head start on our financial positions. The idea is to take some initiative in creating a solid financial foundation, and it has to be better than just working a day job. You will often hear people say, "Well I put in my eight hours today. Time to go home and relax."

If you think that putting in eight hours for somebody else will build a bridge to the land of wealth, then you are in for a rude awakening. How many people do you know who got rich by working for a company for thirty years and then retiring?

Probably not many. I'm talking about rich, not one hundred thousand dollars in a Roth IRA or 401(k) plan. I'm talking about having enough capital to hop on a plane and relocate to a country of your choice for a year. That's being rich to me.

Uncle Sam Wants Your Wallet...I Mean You!

I hope you understand the limitations of devoting all your working hours to your job instead of your financial plan for freedom. The amount of money you could earn is governed by your hourly wage, which is taxed before you even see it in your hands. Can't you see that's a low ceiling on your income? You should be concerned with setting up a business entity whose wealth equation will reward your involvement more favorably.

Be wary of tax laws concerning the wealthy. Go examine your tax records for the last year and read over the forms. Yes, read them over, and see if you can understand the terminology used: capital gains and losses, itemized deductions, head of household, home mortgage interest, rents, royalties, etc.

If you aspire to being well-off or a person of means, then you will greatly benefit from knowing, understanding, and applying the advantages of the tax laws. CPAs—Certified Public Accountants— can greatly assist you with understanding the IRS's financial jargon. Find a smart one in your area and ask lots of questions. When you do find the right one, you will soon realize they are the best teachers for current tax laws.

Education Comes From Educe—Merriam-Webster Defines This As:

1. to bring out (as something latent)

Education is constant; it does not end with a ceremony, tassels, or a diploma in a cheap leather binder. The middle class is continually taxed at higher rates, huh? Well if I were you, I would aspire to get my ass out of that class, step up to the big kids' conference table, where business is conducted, and figure out a way to get smarter than the tax system in this country.

Ever since the dawn of taxes, that is one key trait the wealthy have mastered. Knowing that you can take two hundred and fifty thousand dollars in capital gains profit after staying in your primary residence for two or more years is important to a married person because the amount changes to five hundred thousand dollars if you file jointly with a spouse. Big difference there.

What we really should be taught at an early age is how money works in this country. Why do I care so much about money, you ask? The answer is simple. You will achieve nothing without it.

The desire for riches is simply the capacity for larger life seeking fulfillment; every desire is the effort of an unexpressed possibility to come into action.

—Wallace D. Wattles

Kids should learn and understand the US fiscal system, study its history, and know how to make investments and leverage the tax code in their favor so that they can be ahead of the race, not oblivious to it. Instead we find teaching students how to draw a parabola on a graphing calculator is somehow more important. Geez. Are the "educated" even educated anymore?

Here is a solution for the education system: this book or any other that teaches fundamental financial principles. Maybe it will guide the right minds toward the appropriate paths for financial independence. I look back now and wish I had known of Napoleon Hill when I was thirteen years old and busy learning to play guitar and reading cheesy teenage fiction novels. Maybe I would have liked to have been more responsible for my life and my financial roots.

The good news is I've found something to aspire to in my own life. I started later in life but not as late as others. The idea is to get started; don't put it off. My thing is real estate investment. I could also say providing a home for the American family. Maybe one day I'll be the guy on the other end of the deal, actually taking part in the purchase and not the sale. Perhaps my own American Dream will have come true.

Gambling Is NOT Investing

We see people make millions and lose more than they had in the first place. I've even read the misfortunes of the big lotto winners—maybe not such a golden ticket after all. Tell me this: Why would anyone in the world freely give you five-hundred-and-fifty million dollars? What in the hell makes *you* so special as to be bestowed this amount of money? What value have you provided to people around the world?

What you did was buy a ticket several thousands of times or you "got lucky" and someone gave you a winning ticket. Yeah, that's a laugh. Maybe you like the benefits of the lotteries. "Hey man, they help build our interstate systems and fund our school programs." They'll go on without your hard-earned money. You should be investing it in your business and product. This will pay greater dividends than any investment in lottery tickets or scratch-offs. Hey, I've probably bought more of them than you, so step off my back!

Detach Yourself From Team Self-Indulgence, The Impetus of Consumer Thinking

Invest your time and money wisely. Who the hell cares if you rank at level seventy on *Call of Duty*? Your Xbox buddy right? That's because he's a nobody too. What you could have achieved in reality, you achieved in fantasy play because it was much more convenient from your position on the couch. A sad reality unless you really enjoy the benefits of a being a Xbox war veteran.

I'm not entirely sure what those benefits are, but I'm sure someone could come up with a list if insulted by my words. Just to be clear: I do, in fact, own an Xbox and love it. But I have also realized it's a pastime that doesn't pay me any money unless I'm inventing video games and distributing them to the masses. Catch my drift?

Wake up and realize that the world doesn't care if you're a nice person or have worked hard for so-and-so or such-and-such for beaucoup number of years. Hopefully that doesn't sting too badly. Those are excellent qualities to have as a person but are not of much value in the job marketplace, where potential employers are more interested in tangible skills than years of experience.

Consumers (the majority of people) want a world where they can enjoy themselves and self-indulge their appetites for a while. Flat screen televisions, surround sound, eighteen hundred different channels, and a reality show for every blathering idiot in the world.

Some of those are really cool things no doubt, but look at the investment of your money and, especially, your time. Have you made enough headway in your financial foundation to justify your five-thousand-dollar investment in consumer electronics? How much knowledge can you attain from sabotaging your mind with *Jersey Shore* or other reality TV shows?

The shifting of thought from consumer to producer will hopefully take hold after practicing for a while, and you'll produce new thought patterns that can quickly turn into habits, much like Larry's contribution of ten dollars a week to his savings. He soon forgot about the automatic withdrawals from his checking account, and his savings grew without his involvement.

Plant a seed, or several of them, and watch them grow. It may take a while at first—remember that the ground here is barren and bone-dry. You may need to use the hoe or shovel to break up the surface and loosen the soil underneath. What do you expect? Instantaneous growth? The dirt here is as hard as a brick because you haven't cultivated your financial garden until now. Action will be required on your part to revive the nutrients, and you may have to get your hands dirty.

Freedom of Choice is What You Got

They say that insanity is the result of doing the same thing over and over again and expecting different results. To change your life, start with the small things first, and turn bad habits into good ones.

Instead of blowing that 250 bucks on shots for your pals down at the pub, make a conscious decision that your money belongs elsewhere, like in your pocket, for crying out loud! This is the money you earned for your forty hours of time during the week. I hope that you respect the power and potential behind those two hundred and fifty greenbacks.

If you are not worth a damn at money management, then I suggest some kind of action on your part, whether it be online classes, YouTube videos, financial books, one-on-one counseling and mentoring, seminars, etc. Do something about it. Do not sweep this under the rug! The earlier this lesson can be learned and applied, the sooner it can provide financial cushioning for those just-in-case moments:

⇨ Oh shit, my Honda just threw a rod!

⇨ Dude, my girlfriend's birthday party is tomorrow. I've got to get her a gift or she'll hang me out to dry.

⇨ After attempting to hold a conversation while in the restroom, Joe's cell phone slips and lands in the toilet bowl. Another one bites the dust...

⇨ Todd made several calls to his online girlfriend in American Samoa and now has to pay a four thousand dollar phone bill.

I would personally hate to be caught in any of these situations without some kind of pillow on which to fall, some system with a backup plan. Don't play the victim by finding your financial basket capsized under your supervision. This position is no fun at all, I promise you. Have you ever overdrawn your bank account? It can kill your game quickly and put you in the hole disastrously. Been there and done that.

Expect better of yourself and your peers. You could be a winner in life and still have a losing bank account. The Internet is full of those sad stories and most do not end well. Get your financial well-being under control and have some kind of working plan, one that is sound and realistic. Write it on a napkin and stick it to the fridge or tape it to the dashboard of your car. Engrave it on your toothbrush so you can see it every time you brush those pearly whites.

Riding on the Coattails of Another's Success

The story of Larry is pure fiction but it is a possible scenario nonetheless. Many successful people have allied their forces with growing companies and reap excellent benefits for their investments. Investing is the proverbial hand in the cookie jar, but sometimes you have to wait for those succulent cookies to bake.

If you had the inkling to invest in Apple after 2005, you stood to make a whole lot more money if you rode out the highs and lows. Even in late 2004, for example, shares were trading in the $32 dollar range, compared to the roughly $400 levels they're trading at now. The company has grown exponentially and made their investors rich. What a great scenario: imagine getting in around the thirty-two dollar range and stepping out when the price hit seven hundred dollars a share. That's a 2,087 percent gain!

You can still get in on the idea today. As I write this, Apple's price is in the lower four hundred dollar range, just a minor pullback for the patient investor. Think of it as a growth play, you know the stock has been dragged down but if you are patient price will catch up to true value or you could decide you feel like shorting the stock (I will explain that in the next chapter). Flexibility is your friend.

There are a multitude of other ideas for investment and lots of questions to ask yourself. Should you trade stocks, options, bonds, futures, currencies, or commodities? Maybe you want to invest in real estate. I like that idea too.

Responsibility Eliminates Scapegoats

Invest your time and money into something that pays more than the privilege of bragging about your Xbox live rating or your last Facebook/Twitter status. If you don't make enough money or have trouble paying your bills, such as credit cards and loans, it's time to provide the world with more of your talents and services.

Desire that money runs so deeply through your bank accounts that you can't *give* enough of it away. Why can't this be your reality if you create it? We all start off desiring more than what we have, but we learn best from our parents, don't we? It's natural—they gave us life. We learn most everything from them—understanding of finance, or a lack of understanding of finance.

The thing is, you are not your parents, and you are not your job. You are the sum collection of your thoughts—the body just follows course. You may share certain characteristics with your parents, but they are not you. Life began for you as a single thought, your parents' planned or—oops!—unplanned process of creation (sex + your parents=banish this thought, with haste!)

From that inception you have grown into something all your own, complete with flaws because, let's face it, we're not all like Larry. There's probably a good chance you weren't educated in the realm of financial success. For some reason, it just didn't make it into the syllabus. That's alright because you're here now, seeking a change.

The Spew of Economics Class:

Just wait until you're out there in the real world!

All I remember hearing about back in high school was the "real world." The MTV television program of the same name obviously reflected nothing of the sort, and it became a mystical place to the average teenager. Teachers should tell you that the world doesn't give two shits if you want to be famous musician or a pro athlete. You have to offer people something they want or need and can associate value with.

Anything you can do or imagine doing will take a means of possession, some tradeoff. Time for money. Money for freedoms. The typical transaction usually involves a trade of currency for a chosen product or service. The world is our playground and domain. The more you give to it and enhance others' lives, the more it gives back.

I like to imagine God, or whomever is watching from on high, starts singing Pink Floyd's *Shine On You Crazy Diamond* in my honor—that's just me. We could momentarily stop off at the subject of religion, but I'm afraid that would fill several volumes, and I don't have the time for it at this juncture.

Look around your neighborhood or community. Can you spot any product or service that is needed there? If you can hone your skills and make smart decisions, then you may be well on your way to that one hundred thousand dollar bank account, like Larry's.

If you have musical talents, then you have invested a lot of your time and money into becoming better at your skills. The world is full of musicians—rappers, guitarists, singers, songwriters, drummers, etc. Many of them excel at selling their product or services.

They have set up a mastermind around them to ensure they leverage their time and money. Do you have those things in place? I doubt it. You have to build those relationships. The creative arts are full of people so you better make sure you are more creative than the competition.

Take a deep breath of the oxygen that you freely breathe every day. You are alive, well, and conscientious of your abilities. Know in your heart that you can and will have those things that you most cherish and desire with a burning passion. It is possible and it is real. Once the shift goes from, "How can I be most comfortable today?" to "How can I provide another with comfort and dependable service today?"

The latter thought is sure to set your mind in motion and you may have what experts call "inspired thought." It comes easier with practice. The former thought will only produce the same old lousy results you have been getting: "Why am I broke all the time?" Comfort doesn't breed massive wealth, but massive wealth does breed comfort.

The 400 Richest People in America

Here is more food for thought. I recently read an article on the Yahoo! home page about the four hundred richest people in America. The article stated that the common trend among these people were that they all made nearly half of their income from capital gains.

The capital gains tax laws have lightened since the 1990s and any information concerning capital gains is very important for any investor. Depending on your tax bracket, you can pay anywhere from 0 to 15 percent in taxes on long term capital gains. Short term gains (day traders, swing traders) are taxed as ordinary income.

The Fortunate 400 discussed in the article started off with small gains and invested those funds back into their portfolios and, henceforth, became richer. The more money you have to leverage, the more substantial the gains and/or losses.

If you want to be rich, model these four hundred people's common habit of investing, whether it's in stocks, real estate, or your own product. Find what fits you and learn it extremely well. Learn how supply and demand works, and understand the impacts of certain events on your investments.

Formulate and stamp indelibly on your mind a mental picture of yourself as succeeding. Hold this picture tenaciously. Never permit it to fade. Your mind will seek to develop the picture...Do not build up obstacles in your imagination.

—Norman Vincent Peale

V. PROTECTING THOSE

INVESTMENTS

The individual investor should act consistently as an investor and not as a speculator. This means... that he should be able to justify every purchase he makes and each price he pays by impersonal, objective reasoning that satisfies him that he is getting more than his money's worth for his purchase.

—Benjamin Graham

Woes of Wall Street

If you have a boatload of cash, then please be careful where you invest your funds. I know everyone has heard the stock market horror stories. Many people took to jumping off high-rise buildings after the crash of 1929. Stocks were purchased on margin—borrowed money from the broker. Losses exceeded the borrowers' available capital…and mental deterioration steps in when you can't swallow the pill of owing the brokerage house a hefty sum of money.

The bull market had fooled the American public into thinking it could possibly go on forever. People were borrowing heavily to invest in the stock market, trying to strike it rich. Nothing is so misleading as giving a little and expecting to reap a mother lode in return.

You have to remember this was before the U.S. Securities and Exchange Commision (SEC) was created to regulate Wall Street's affairs (1934) and also before the Glass-Steagall Act (also called the Banking Act of 1933) came into effect, which set up the FDIC, regulated commercial and investment banking, and set restrictions on *speculative* bank activities. The Depression made it necessary to address the reason why the country was in a slump and set up laws to protect it from happening again.

Jesse Livermore, world renown stock market trader during the early 1900s, said never meet a margin call and never average down in buying—which means adding to a position whose price has dropped below your market entry point. Any books concerning his trading style and techniques

(*Reminiscences of a Stock Operator, How to Trade in Stocks*) give great insight into the mind of a successful trader.

Exercising Control: You Can't Control Which Direction a Stock Moves, but You Can Exit and Save Face

Don't raise a blind eye to your investments, whatever they may be. If the price moves against you and you are uncomfortable with it, liquidate the position immediately. Don't put up with any shit from a stock—make a move and tell yourself that you are in control of what happens to your money, not it. If the behavior of the stock turns more favorable, you can always get back in at a later date.

At this point you are just observing, making speculations about stock direction and general market direction. Let those ideas brew and see what happens. How many times are you wrong about the short-term direction of a given stock? How many times are you right? This is important to do before you place any orders. Get the feel of things and you might develop a knack for trading.

Good traders have a special talent for trading just as good musicians and good athletes have talents for their fields. Great traders are ones who are absorbed by the talent. They don't have the talent—the talent has them.

—Ed Seykota, as quoted in *Market Wizards*

The cool thing about the markets is the diversity of trading opportunities available. You can buy securities or you can sell them. Do you think the company will do well? Then buy shares at a low entry point to get a feel for the stock behavior. If the stock price continues to rise, increase your number of shares. Traders have coined this term pyramiding.

Short Selling

If you think the company's share price will decline, sell the stock short. You don't purchase shares but borrow them from your broker instead and sell them on the open market. At some point you must "buy to cover" your position—you must purchase the shares you borrowed so you can return them to your broker. You hope for a decline in price so that the difference between your entry point and exit point is favorable.

For example, you borrow one hundred shares of XYZ from your broker and sell them at ten dollars a share, giving you a one-thousand dollar credit. The stock is slaughtered by continuous selling, driving the stock down to seven dollars a share. You buy one hundred shares at this price to cover your position (return the shares you borrowed from the broker) or close out the trade. The result is a profit of three hundred dollars, minus trading commissions, interest, and fees.

Discount brokerage house commissions will vary. Lately I've seen $3.95 and up for most trades. Many of these brokers offer incentives for signing up—sixty free trades, fifty bucks for each referral, complimentary bragging rights, etc. Check some different ones out and see what you have to do to apply for the offers—they will likely want you to fund your account with a minimum of five hundred to one thousand dollars to take advantage of the deals.

You want to invest in companies that are growing locally, domestically, and globally. See the brand in Hong Kong? That's fantastic. Don't concern yourself with the hot penny stock newsletters and their magnificent gains. If someone truly knew what direction a stock was headed, why would they tell the world? What benefit would they gain from it?

Make your own investment decisions and, when you strike a million in the markets, you can have the privilege of saying you got rich through your wise investment choices, not from some hot tip or advice. It was the hard work and patience you put in—your money management skills and discipline. There's not a mystical formula for success. You have to work at it.

You become a millionaire because you take the initiative to recognize the changing trends in your locale and you seek to make money with that information. It would be useless brain material without some kind of benefit, yes?

Focus on What You Can Control

Then you add to your positions as they rise in value, always protected by a physical stop-loss or mental alarm (I've found most brokers will also let you set price alerts that can notify you via text message!) Before you buy a stock, determine your exit point, unless you plan to hold it forever (Buffett strategy). What is the absolute maximum loss that you would tolerate? I know you wouldn't take any crap from anybody in life so why take it from a stock?

Don't become furious with a losing position—take action. Sell off all or half your shares to reduce your exposure if you become uneasy about the position. Sometimes your intuition, feelings, and assumptions about a stock's behavior will be wrong—there is no question about it. As human beings we don't like accepting that we may be wrong about things—people, perceptions, or a stock's direction—from time to time. The ego sometimes throws tantrums so watch out.

Understand that you can control your emotions. If you say you can't or won't take responsibility for that, then maybe you're in the wrong field of opportunity. Real estate may appeal more to your taste. Before undertaking any trading, I would strongly recommend reading into psychology and human behavior. If you have an understanding of how the market's biggest operators (individuals, money managers, and computer programs crafted by humans) work, you may to start to grasp why things tick the way they do.

Once you are in the markets, your mind can become saturated with the numbers floating around your head and you may start to notice patterns or trends. From there, it's accurately predicting which direction the stock will go and then putting your money where your mouth is.

Capital Gains/Losses: The Best Teachers For Trading

There are all kinds of trading enthusiasts. There are day traders who make several orders in a day, the swing traders whose investment time frames range from a day to two weeks, and then the longer-term investors who don't plan to make many orders—maybe two or three—in the course of a year.

What they have in common is that they all pay taxes on capital gains, which are considered short-term when the investment is held for under one year, and is taxed at regular income levels. If the investment is held for two years or better, then it is considered a long-term capital gain, meaning you pay less than regular income taxes, and sometimes pay no capital gains tax at all if you are just now starting out with a lower income.

Here's what I've gathered from my own observations in the market. I've had an operating account since August 2010 and from the trades I've made—both winning and losing—I've gathered this information from my trading notes (very wise idea if you like learning from your mistakes).

My best winners were holds of one to three days. The moderate gains were made in five to eighteen trading days and the nasty losers came from the times when I incessantly held on to hope and chance while ignoring the basic trend that steadily decimated my position day after hopeful day. Another thing: the majority of my trades have given me a few opportunities to sneak out with either a small profit or at least break-even prices. Don't let greed override your logic and reasoning skills!

Recommendations

I'll go ahead and throw a few of these out there at you because maybe my mistakes will not be yours. I learned some things the hard way, as most important lessons are learned, I suppose.

That's why I say to read as many books on investing as possible. I'm not saying this will make you insanely rich—although it has the potential to—but when you have enough capital via your other investments, such as real estate or business, the markets can operate as your wealth preservation tool. It's easier to generate bigger returns with a bigger trading account, and that's why you should begin investing with your small money. When the big money comes your way, you'll know exactly how to preserve it and watch it take off like Jack's beanstalk.

If you want to day trade, read some books by active day traders. It takes a winner with rock-hard discipline to survive in today's fast-paced markets. You have to adapt to change when it comes, almost like a chameleon, blending into your surroundings until the moment investment potential starts to rise up.

There are multiple trading ideas to consider. The simplest I can think of is buying shares of an ETF that tracks the performance of any of the major indexes such as NASDAQ, Standard & Poor's, Russell 2000, or the Dow Jones Industrial Average. They even offer ETFs that are for shorting the index, if you happen to feel bearish (bears think downward trends, bulls go for upward trends).

Maybe you aren't partial to stocks. Check out the options market then. They trade much like stocks do, except they are cheaper to trade and expiration dates accompany them. No buy and hold here. This area has been growing with heavy volume ever since the option contracts market was introduced early in the 1970s.

Investing for Life

For anyone wanting to become an investor, understand that investing is a lifelong endeavor and that you may have to make adjustments to your lifestyle, but the reward in a few short years could really open up new avenues of wealth.

Ever heard of accredited investors? These are natural people with one million dollars in net worth—not including their primary residences—or who have made over two hundred thousand dollars in income each of the two most recent years. The rules may be different in other countries, so let's keep it stateside. There are other ways to become an accredited investor. Visit www.sec.gov/answers/accred.htm to see if you apply.

These people open up their investments to new avenues of wealth that are not permitted for the everyday investor. If you don't have a million put away and you don't apply to be an accredited investor in the United States, then you are stuck with the same investment options as the general public. To be accredited is to have the big opportunities presented to *you* because you have applied yourself and your talents enough to know that money can work for you and grow into something much larger and rewarding.

Whatever funds you trade with should not affect your everyday life if you lose them. Like I said before, if you become uncomfortable with the position, *sell*. Don't hope it will come back. The markets don't care if you hope for anything at all. They are fueled by fear and greed, two emotions that are unrelenting to hope's walls of defense. Occasionally optimism will shine for whatever reason—consumers are spending more money, interest rates or gas prices are at record lows, high employment rates, or simply lots of folks are buying stocks—and we'll have a fantastic bull market.

Remember This!

You can make as much money as you set your mind to make. Believe that, and accept it as fact. Keep your mind closed tightly against all negativity. Some people have lost sight of their dreams and they certainly don't want to be alone in that venture. Misery loves company. Stay away from this crowd and begin to live your life as you see fit. You can escape mediocrity and the mundane realities of the rat race.

VI. SETTING UP A

BROKERAGE ACCOUNT

Everyone has the brainpower to follow the stock market. If you made it through fifth-grade math, you can do it.

—Peter Lynch.

What's This Woodshed You Speak Of, Mr. Broker?

I know it sounds fancy, doesn't it? Think about it, your own personal broker who you can ring up during market hours and say, "Buy! Buy! Buy!" or "Sell! Sell! Sell!" if it should happen to turn against you. Many options and services are provided in the financial markets. We have, for instance, the bigger full-service brokerage houses—Morgan Stanley, Charles Schwab, Merrill Lynch, and Edward Jones, to name a few.

Their employees have educated themselves in financial instruments and often hold MBAs and have titles such as financial advisor, planner, or consultant. I'm sure they are all great establishments. I actually took part in the construction of one of these firms in my area and I know they are lovely places to visit. You may notice their offices are exquisitely adorned with cherry or mahogany woodwork and furniture, gold plaques, Evian water, etc. You can pick this option and relinquish control of your financial destiny, leaving it with the people who have expertise in these areas. Not a bad option, but maybe you prefer one more suited to your own needs.

Discount Brokers: Frugalians Go Crazy!

Discount brokerage houses are often less adorned and, in this arena, you are more on your own when picking investments. Brokers can assist with trades but not always freely. Many of them provide valuable trading tools that are made available online through their websites. Some will have offices, but not necessarily in your vicinity. Here's a few to get you started:

⇨ E*TRADE (with the cute talking-baby commercials)

⇨ Scottrade

⇨ TradeKing (recently merged with Zecco)

⇨ MB Trading

⇨ Fidelity Investments

⇨ optionsXpress (acquired by Charles Schwab in 2011)

⇨ TD Ameritrade

You must be 18 years of age or older to start one by yourself and if you are younger than that, you can have your parents or guardian help you get started investing with a custodial account. There are a multitude of options and commissions for each of these. Find the one that suits your needs. Check out FindtheBest at: brokerage-accounts.findthebest.com. You can weigh out the pros and cons of each brokerage firm and pick one that fits your style.

Chances are you'll have to relay some important information to these establishments, such as your social security number, address, and mother's maiden name, mostly for tax purposes and security. Don't be afraid. Yes, it takes time to set up, so set aside a spot in your busy schedule for it. Make it happen, no excuses.

Many of these firms are competing for new customers so they may offer sixty free trades for sixty days, or something along those lines, to attract new traders. My online broker has offered fifty dollars for every referral that funds an account with three thousand dollars. That's fifty dollars for me and for my friend. Like I said, find one that fits your style and run with it. If you have enough money, you can switch firms every month to take advantage of all the startup offers.

Entrepreneur's Logic: I Control My Future

The tax laws and codes in this country are set up to work in the favor of the people who understand them and leverage every opportunity made available. Where do we find a lot of wealthy people? In government positions maybe? Think about it. If the Internal Revenue Service (IRS) can collect twenty percent or more of your paycheck, then nothing will change that unless you make a rational decision that you will not accept this. Quit your job and find something more profitable to engage your mind and time in. That should really put a fire under your ass.

Many people have had the courage to face these fears—*How will I ever pay the bills without a* job?—and step out on faith (according to sba.gov there were twenty-seven million small businesses in 2010). This allows the input of fresh ideas.

Let's say you did it. Who knows? Something wonderful might happen. Quitting your job has the potential to change the entire course of your life, so think about that for a while. Entrepreneurial roads and opportunities can be found anywhere and everywhere you look. We live in a world where organized and brilliantly executed ideas are worth more than anything you could ever type up on a job résumé.

It has been said that nothing in this world is necessarily good or evil. The only thing that does matter is the meaning or emotional state we apply to it. How does something make you feel?—Good, bad, resentful, ecstatic, angry, relieved, at ease? If you approach everything with an open mind and a clear conscience, you can produce favorable outcomes.

You can see the train from both sides of the track, from not just one vantage point but several, so you can weigh the pros and cons more efficiently and you won't risk being blindsided when another locomotive comes barreling down the track, which happens sometimes whether we like it or not. Don't complain. Learn the lesson and build from that experience.

Financially Advise Yourself

Now that you have set up a brokerage account, you are on the road to making your own investment decisions, paving the way for your financial future. Can you get rich in the stock market? Absolutely, but it will take rock-hard discipline and the ability to learn and adapt quickly. The markets are ever-changing and few make it.

What you are doing with your trading is learning the ropes early, when your funds are minimal, so that when your funds become exponential—when you write the next *Harry Potter* or *Fifty Shades of Grey* or create a grilled-cheese sandwich maker that sells on the Home Shopping Network—you can preserve your wealth and watch it grow faster than ever before.

When you fund your account with those hard-earned dollars, letting them now go to work for *you*, you are sustaining your future. The money seed has finally taken to the ground, and you have a money tree with a developing root system. Its nutrients come from where you have placed your money and time.

Please be cautious and learn as much as you can before actually doing any buying or selling in the markets. Preservation of funds is absolutely critical to your success. Do not haphazardly or lackadaisically watch your funds melt before your eyes like butter in a hot skillet. Always protect your capital. If you are left without it, you'll have a brokerage account with no funds to trade—an entirely worthless position to be in. Learn your lessons quickly and be able to adapt to the changes in the markets.

You should realize that Wall Street will always have a tuition fee. Why do you think most people avoid it? (*Wait a sec...you mean I can lose money? There's no way I'm doing that!*) No reason to be angry about it. It's the price of playing the game. To play smart and win is to think safe investments, companies that have the potential to grow fifty to three hundred percent in the next five years.

The chances of winning enormously, of hitting a grand slam out of the park, are greater in the smaller companies because the big institutions don't have their hands in the cookie jar yet, so allocate a small percentage of your funds to speculative plays. You can also lose enormously with the smaller companies, if they should hit rough patches or dissolve, so the amount of money you put in these speculative companies is entirely up to you as an intelligent and disciplined investor.

One of my rules of thumb for trading in speculative companies is I like to see an average of three-hundred thousand trades (volume) during market hours. New York markets are open Monday thru Friday, 9:30 a.m. to 4 p.m. EST, except for U.S. holidays. There are also pre-market (7 a.m. to 9:30 a.m.) and after hours (4:00 p.m. to 8:00 p.m.) trading sessions for die-hard enthusiasts.

I want you to have a general idea of what you're up against when investing in stocks. Always have some exit point, be it a particular day, quote price, or piece of news—unless you plan on holding it forever, known as the Buffett model. Set a maximum loss you are willing to tolerate and stick to it. Remember that you want to preserve capital as much as possible so that you can invest further and get richer.

Financial Literacy: Talking the Talk

Hit up the local library and check out as many books on investing as they will allow you. This book is intended as a starting point, not the end of your investing journey. I asked a librarian how many books I could have out at one time. She said she knew of someone who had checked out about ninety over the course of a few days. Can you beat that?

Make a commitment to yourself to read as much as you have to before the information becomes second nature to you and slips into your conversations time and again. You can talk the talk now. *Hey, honey, I just placed a market order to buy one thousand shares of Esoteric Semiconductor.*

You know what calls and puts are. You understand the difference between assets and liabilities, fundamental and technical investing. You've read about buying on margin, DRIPs, IPOs, EPS ratios, support/resistance levels, dollar-cost averaging, market capitalization, interest rates, IRAs, stock splits, etc.

You can, and have, successfully placed market orders, even though you lean more towards the limit order, trailed by a 10 percent stop-loss order. Nicolas Darvas said his most important tool was the stop-loss order, which he employed with all his orders. His dance show took him to the far corners of the world, from Hong Kong to Istanbul, so he made it mandatory to have a physical limit or exit point on his investments.

You can't know whether you are wrong or right until the moment your money is on the table. Like I have said before, invest in those companies that are growing exponentially and the ones whose products are everywhere—TV, magazines, e-mails, billboards. You want the surest, most favorable odds of success when your money is on the line.

Learning From the Pioneers of Trading

While I'm here, I should tell you to pick up Edwin LeFèvre's book, *Reminiscences of a Stock Operator*. It's the fictionalized account of Jesse Livermore's trading and work ethics, and a look into the life of a phenomenal trader whose life ended abruptly. He made and lost millions at least four different times in his trading career and has said that he lost those same millions by not adhering to the discipline that made him a fortune on "the Street."

Jesse Livermore certainly had the picturesque life of the Wall Street trader of the early 1900s, makes me think of F. Scott Fitzgerald's *The Great Gatsby*. His life was totally immaculate and grandiose to the outside eye: mansion on the water, house servants, and a personal yacht to the mainland every morning. Things did not end well for him—read his *How to Trade Stocks* with updates by Richard Smitten for a more in-depth look at his life.

Another investor that should pique your interest is Warren Buffett, often referred to as the *Oracle of Omaha* or the greatest investor of our time. His trading secret is none other than buying into companies that he perceives as undervalued—simple and very profitable for Mr. Buffett. He typically does not sell unless there's good reason to do so.

There is a core reason behind his success and that may be why people trust him with their money. Would you feel safe putting your money with Warren's company (Berkshire Hathaway), whose share price is the highest on the exchange? At the close of trading on December 31, 2012, the price stood at $134,060 a share! That was 0.80 percent up for the day, or $1,060 in the green.

What I would suggest to any trader who aspires to be great at this game is to start checking successful companies out, one by one. Call up their investor relations departments and probe them for information. Maybe they have a pamphlet or a sample of their product to try—sometimes you get lucky. Yahoo! Finance is my go to information source for screening potential company's stock.

Ask yourself if they have a sustainable business model that can survive dubious and sluggish times. Think like an entrepreneur and a business owner—successful traders and investors understand the game in which they play. They have a feel for it because they have ridden out the waves of fluctuation, which are inevitable in today's brisk markets.

My goal was to hit stocks that would make the biggest possible percentage gains, because I have long realized that I can't always hit right. Therefore, what I must do is to manage my speculations in such a way that when I lose, I lose only a little; and when I win, I win big!

—Nicolas Darvas

Stalking Your Chosen Stocks

The first investment tool I employed was the watch list my broker provided to me. I check out my company's trading activities daily to better understand the flow and general direction of the market. At the time, the app for my iPhone wasn't all that great, and I wanted fast and updated quotes in real time so I could genuinely follow my chosen stock's trading.

I did some digging and found the CNBC Real-Time app to be the most intriguing and informative. Here you can add your favorite companies, get updated real-time quotes, and watch informative videos from top trading experts. *Mad Money* and all the other great shows are updated daily, and there should be an abundance of ideas to immerse your trading opportunist mind in.

Traders today have so many more advantages and subsequent pitfalls than they did fifty years ago. With the furthering of technology, we have the ability to liquidate quickly if the need should arise. Your entire trading can now be enjoyed anywhere, right from your mobile phone or laptop. Wherever you are in the world, you always have access to your accounts—unless you take a spontaneous vacation to the Arctic Circle.

Currency and Charts

Could global trading be your niche? Forex (foreign exchange markets) traders can, and often do, trade around the clock because, somewhere, a market is running—London and New York closes, Tokyo and Australia markets open. It's almost 24/7 trading, with the exception of weekends!

Another essential part of trading is the ability to read charts (Quick-Charts has developed a great app for traders on the go.) There are only three ways in which stock can ride—up, down, or sideways (stagnant activity). Can you identify which direction a stock is headed? If you can, then you can make a wager on your convictions.

Check out Japanese candlestick charts for a more exposed view of what is driving the stock. You'll be happy to know they are much easier on the eyes than traditional bar and line charts. StockCharts.com provides a good look at some of the different patterns: stockcharts.com/school/doku. php?id=chart_school:chart_analysis:introduction_to_candlesticks

The main point is that there is a plethora of information at your fingertips so use it. The twenty-first century provides the typical American household with cable, phone, Internet, and satellite—four possible sources of valuable information. There's only one problem. You have the remote in your hand. What could you possibly learn and apply from watching an all-week marathon of *House*? A bunch of useless medical babble? Where the hell are people's priorities these days?

Realize that every one of us has something to give or contribute to this world, something which makes life easier or better in some way. Find yours and cultivate it. Treasure it and let it out into the world so it may keep on giving.

VII. Buying That

First House

It's tangible, it's solid, it's beautiful. It's artistic, from my standpoint, and I just love real estate.

—Donald Trump

Mortgages and Retirement

I guess it's your turn to take a nosedive off the deep end and strap that one-hundred-thousand-dollar—or better—debt to your back. What comes next? Marriage, kids, sponge baths at the retirement home?

Let me ask you a serious question: Does retiring at age sixty-five really sound all that and a bag of peaches to you? Can you see yourself frolicking on the beach half-naked when your hair is grey and you have to drink prune juice to have regular bowel movements? Does that sound like reality? Who do you see at the beach when you go? Think about it. Let me put it like this: Who do you *want* to see at the beach when you go?

I don't know about you, but I would rather enjoy retirement as early as I possibly can. I don't want to slave away at an eight-to-five job for the rest of my life. That doesn't sound appealing or motivating to me at all. What does sound appealing is a career metamorphosis into self employment before my thirties so I can concentrate on my real dreams and goals: real estate investment and letting my money go to work for me now.

Do I think it's possible to retire early? Yes, many people have achieved it and lived to write books about it. I've read enough stories from aspiring entrepreneurs to ascertain the fact in my own mind.

Larry Land-Owner

Our good buddy Larry has decided it's the right time to purchase a home, but he's torn on the location. There's the bachelor pad on the beach with an eight hundred dollar a year increase in property taxes and insurance or the three-bedroom, two-bath house in the up-and-coming subdivision. Ahhh…choices, choices.

He picks the house in the suburbs because of the savings and also because his diligent research shows that the schools in the area achieved the highest test scores in the county. Home buyers, and especially families with kids, pay attention to that stuff when home shopping. Wal-Mart was built close by and several new businesses have followed suit—convenience stores, banks, and sushi bars. Driving consumers who are looking for housing in the area are new industries and along with it, thousands of jobs.

What Larry has really done is invest his money into a growing neighborhood. If the community continues to grow at present rates, then he's sure he can almost double his money on the house. He also plans to stay in the house for at least two years to take advantage of the capital gains tax law for real estate.

After living two or more years in your primary residence, you can keep up to two hundred and fifty thousand dollars in profits when you sell if you file as a single person, and five hundred thousand dollars if you're married. That's an authentic golden nugget right there.

Larry plans to improve the property during his stay—whatever will bring the house up to modern living standards. He regularly picks up the *Dream Kitchens & Baths* magazine from the local home improvement store and scans it for new ideas to benefit and improve his investment. He starts with small projects first: new paint, blinds and curtains, faucets, and light fixtures—the rather inexpensive solutions that can make a huge difference in appearance. Nothing over the top really, just something different and vibrant.

Other houses in his neighborhood sell for twenty-five thousand dollars more than he purchased his for, and he knows he made a wise investment that will one day provide a home for a beautiful couple or budding family. In two years, the market in your area could become highly desirable (If you did your research and due diligence then you already know this.) All you need to do is provide a home eloquently.

Real Estate Investing: Having a Plan Comes First!

From the start, Larry conceived a plan for the house, one that he wrote down and studies consistently. He plans on putting a 20 percent down payment on the house to avoid paying PMI (private mortgage insurance), which is basically insurance on behalf of your broker in the event that you default on the loan. He begins to draw up his diagram for success.

⇨ Establish credit and attain an excellent credit score/rating

⇨ Get checked out and preapproved by a reputable mortgage company

⇨ Find a real estate agent who meets his personal needs and knows his area

⇨ Start scouting and surveying potential properties

⇨ Find a great home in a growing location

⇨ Buy, improve the property, sell in two years

⇨ Repeat formula and seek to quantify it

This is sure to produce a favorable amount of wealth. Not quickly—think Internet for quick wealth—but it can certainly add to your overall net worth.

Real estate is the only investment I can think of that has value beyond the asking price—more than gold and silver (I've heard enough of those annoying commercials instructing people to cash in their used gold for extra cash.) It's rentable, salable, leasable, and buyable, can be zoned for business, commercial or industrial use, subdivided and sold in plots to developers, etc.

What if I found gold veins and deposits in my backyard? Although it isn't probable, it is most certainly not impossible. Guess which country is the only one to allow their citizens to own the minerals beneath their property? Good ole U.S. of America baby! What would happen to the value of my investment then? Dare to dream big, oh dreamer of the world!

Consider this. Much of the earth's gold is at the core and is believed to have been deposited there by meteorites around 3.9 billion years ago. It has been found in California, Alaska, Australia, and a decent chunk of it is still being mined at the Witwatersrand Basin in South Africa. I have to wonder is gold a gift from outer space? God's sense of humor at work?

Hey there good people of the world. God here. You know, the Creator? Yeah... look here's some gold I accidentally smashed into the earth when I was moving the furniture around a few billion years ago. All you have to do is figure out how to extract it and profit by it. Gotta run, I'm playing a round of golf with Simon Peter around 9:00 and then back to business as usual. Hasta luego!

Fear not, little flock: for it is your Father's good pleasure to give you the kingdom.

—St. Luke 12: 32 (KJV)

Offering the World a Finished Product

Larry's formula for success is my own personal blueprint for the steps I took in purchasing a home. The entire process will take a few years, but that's fine with me because I'm a patient guy. Understand that by doing these things early, you can avoid any major setbacks along the way.

Most people want to buy a finished product, not something they have to fix up and sink money into. That's your job, remember? They want a dependable, reliable house that will last them for years, and the great thing is that they are willing to pay you for it. You weathered the sheetrock dust and ugly walls for a while, sacrificed your comfort today for another's comfort down the road.

Consumer to producer. Flip the tracks and live how you want to, but with a financial plan and the discipline that goes along with it. Live with a definite chief aim, a destination you aspire to travel to one day, a burning desire for great things, and riches with which to enjoy them. You can begin to focus on abundance and riches, never on the lack of them.

Whatever you want to do and how you want to achieve it will begin to merge into one. You see, you are becoming this image of the character you hold in your mind.

Success requires no apologies, failure permits no alibis.
—Napoleon Hill

My Pursuit of Credit During a Credit Crisis

Sometime around 2009 when I decided to invest my money in real estate, I saw "for sale" signs everywhere I went. All I heard on the news were stories about the recession, the stock market crash, or the growing number of foreclosures in the United States. This bank merged with that bank. Bailouts were issued by the government for multiple organizations, including such big names as General Motors, Goldman Sachs, Citigroup, AIG, Chrysler, Wells Fargo, Bank of America, and JPMorgan Chase.

Mortgage interest rates were low at the time—around 4.5 percent when I finally locked in for my house. That is great for buyers. (They went even lower and are around 3.5% as of May 2013.) The interest rates for a bank savings account sucked royal ass because the government wanted consumers spending their money, not saving it and making that huge 0.03 percent dividend every month.

In the course of my time working offshore, I had paid off all my student loans and other debts that weighed on my mind. I didn't want anything to hold me back from financial freedom. When I finally found a house I thought was a good deal, I inquired about it, only to be denied because I had no credit history.

I had paid everything off and, therefore, had no revolving credit for the lending agencies to see or evaluate on my credit report. Seeing that you paid off your bills early is not good enough for these folks. They want to see you have the responsible habit of paying all your debts monthly, on time, every time.

At the time my bank wouldn't give me a credit card because I didn't have enough credit history to deem me reliable, even though my account housed twenty thousand dollars of my hard earned money for them to lend at prime rates. I was pissed and withdrew my money not long after.

I talked to my dad about my financial problems; he's a pretty smart guy that knows how to solve problems. Soon afterward, we made a trip to his bank, where I was introduced to a pleasant woman who was also a definite problem solver. The solution was a three-thousand dollar CD (certificate of deposit) bought by me in which the borrower was the securer of the loan. In other words, I put up my own money.

The bank then gave me a cashier's check for three thousand dollars to do with what I pleased. I put it in a checking account and automatically made my payments for the loan online every month. Why couldn't my bank come up with this solution? Yes, I ultimately paid interest on the loan, somewhere around 160 dollars I believe, which was a minimal fee to get the ball rolling on my credit.

A year or two later, I was preapproved by a mortgage lender and referred to a local realtor. When you find one who understands your investment objectives, that person will be your best friend. You build relationships that can continue to grow on their own, creating an alliance or brotherhood of people working toward a common objective.

In the mix is your banker (loan officer), mortgage broker, insurance agent, realtor, other investors, contractor or tradesmen, and, of course, yourself. You may find people who are essentially doing the same thing, what is nowadays called "flipping houses."

Buy a house, improve it, sell it for a profit. It can be done, and has been done, by many people. I've been to the real estate guru seminars, and they accelerate their deals by forming beneficial relationships with other wealthy professionals in their field. No secret there.

Nothing-Down Real Estate

Can you purchase real estate with no money down? Sure you can. Would I advise it? Hell no. That road is riddled with disease and decay. It's called the treasonous path of large debt. The only way I want a large debt is when I'm sitting comfortably on enough money to pay it off and continue my selfish lifestyle with no bumps in the road.

Your alliance or team are your top prospects, your main vein to success in real estate. Make sure they understand your investment criterion and objectives because they are the ones swinging the bat for you. Next thing on the agenda is to get your ass out there and start looking. Many houses have "for sale" signs up, but I like finding the mysterious no-sign homes—adds a certain thrill to the search I guess.

Foreclosures are quickly becoming the next epidemic, especially since the financial crash of 2008 to 2009. Let me ask you a question while I'm here, dancing around the subject. Why are there so many foreclosures? Have you thought about it?

Homeowners defaulted on their loans because they had put little or no money down on the property and had no way to pay the hefty mortgage— obviously a bad decision by both lender and borrower of said mortgage— and nobody to sell to because prices were over-inflated when the houses were purchased.

Remember that when you hear a no-money down infomercial for real estate on the radio. It can be done, but I wouldn't recommend leveraging an insane amount of debt unless you're a millionaire, and then I say go ahead.

Here are some websites of market listings that I have found useful:

⇨ Zillow (www.zillow.com)

⇨ Trulia (www.trulia.com)

⇨ Realtor.com (www.realtor.com)

⇨ Gulf Coast MLS (www.gulfcoastMLS.com)

Due Diligence: Reconnaissance and Getting Hands-On

These websites show you valuable information, including what price the house sold for in recent years, nearby home sales, schools in the area, calculators to break down your payments, etc. Think of this as your warm-up exercise. The real fun begins when you actually go and visit a property.

There are sure to be a few surprises: fleas—those ubiquitous and malicious bastards—big dogs not on leashes, snakes chasing after you, homeless people, busted sewer pipes, birds in the laundry vent, etc. Trust me, you will run into your own surprises when you begin to get out there and look around.

Make sure to walk around the property and talk to anybody who'll listen in the neighborhood. Ask questions. People love to talk, especially about their homes—it's where they spend a huge portion of their waking life. Spot any cop cars in the driveways? How about idling at the curb, waiting to arrest the local drug lord? Are the neighbors noisy? Does the yard flood when it rains and, if so, how quickly does it drain?

These are important questions to ask when house hunting. Does the house come with appliances and, if so, do they work? How old is the water heater? Visit properties with a notepad and pen in hand to jot down ideas and facts about the house so you can refer back to them later.

Get familiar with the basic components and systems of a house because you will be the one maintaining the property. Learn a few basic plumbing skills and have a working knowledge of electrical components. Can you patch a hole in sheetrock, change out a faucet, and unclog a drain? If not, are you financially capable of hiring a contractor, tradesmen, or a friend to repair these things for you?

Always check out an attic or basement. You want to see if there is any structural damage or leaks you need to be aware of. How well is it insulated, if at all? Any old wiring or plumbing that may require skilled contractors? This is your due diligence phase and if you find any potential problems, you can get estimates and talk to your realtor about any problems that may need to be addressed before making a bid.

The bank has stipulations on what they will and will not finance considering it's either an investment property or your own personal residence. If you're capable of full cash offers, most likely no one will bat an eye at you if the bathroom is missing a toilet or the roof is leaking.

Holy Homeowner!

Buying a home is a big investment—investment meaning you can liquidate for a higher price than you paid. If you are serious about taking on a mortgage, than have at least 10 percent to put down on the house and if you have 20 or even 40 percent, hooray for you. This means you won't have to pay PMI (private mortgage insurance). I like having money down on the property so it means more to me than just a house with four walls.

Defaulting on a loan should never be an option. By this time you should have done all your homework on the house and considered it a wise investment of your time, money, and efforts. Retreat is not an option. Be prepared for any possible worst-case scenarios. Go ahead and move forward with your plan, never doubting its manifestation in your life. Don't be inundated by fear or doubts. Trust in yourself, always.

Life, the magical musing genius, enjoys rewarding those who know that they can have what they want and are willing to pay whatever price they must to have it. It's do or do not. Once your mind is made up and you have stepped forward in faith and certainty, then life will have your back. You have shown great courage and resistance to the status quo and want something else for your life.

Until one is committed, there is hesitancy, the chance to draw back. Concerning all acts of initiative (and creation), there is one elementary truth that ignorance of which kills countless ideas and splendid plans: that the moment one definitely commits oneself, then Providence moves too.

—William Hutchinson Murray

What we are trying to achieve with a 10 or 20 percent down payment is an establishment of equity in the house and a lower monthly payment. You want your overall financial position to be healthy so people can appreciate you and want to work with you. When these people see you are preapproved and looking to fork over thousands of dollars on a house, they know you are serious and not some hack. Treat them like the professionals they are, and they will return the favor.

The team you assemble could look something like this:

⇨ You, the investor

⇨ Family, friends, mutual investors

⇨ Accountant

⇨ Real estate lawyer

⇨ Insurance agent

⇨ Realtor

⇨ Mortgage broker

⇨ Skilled contractors and tradesmen

Profit From Problems

Buying a house requires a team effort and you will owe these people for their patience, hard work, and willingness to work with you. If you consistently invest in worthwhile and profitable ventures, then people will start to catch on and want to side with you in your investments. They are really making an investment in you and in your ability to follow through with your plans.

If you think you can succeed by yourself, then maybe you can. But first observe actresses, actors, directors, or producers who have received awards for their contributions to blockbuster movies. You will hear them thanking multiple people in succession, as though they have memorized a list before attending. They understand that their success would not have been possible without the right team backing them. No one wins alone.

Reach out and inspire others to change their lives too. If they are comfortable, then who would blame them for not taking action? If you or anyone else has any complaint whatsoever about anything, then you have a chance to change your thinking and, ultimately, your life. Will you solve this problem or let it linger in hopes it will somehow magically work itself out?

The problem is that the majority of people will take the path of least resistance—ignoring the problem and forgetting about it, never taking action and responsibility for their lives. Rest assured the complaint department will be back in full swing soon.

Here's how it is. Let's say you have a complaint. You have a problem that you feel _____ about (fill in the blank with whatever emotion is tantalizing your bloodstream.) Let's hear some common examples:

⇨ "I overdrew my bank account for the fourth time."

⇨ "Looks like I'm on the broke train yet again."

⇨ "How are we going to pay the rent?"

⇨ "Man, I'm so sleepy."

All of these are classic examples, some of which you may have encountered in the past seventy-two hours. From now on we'll entertain some new thoughts and problem solving solutions.

Problem #1

"I overdrew my bank account for the fourth time."

Hold right there in your chair so I can come and slap you on the wrist again. You've been such a bad, bad little pupil! Go to your room and sit in the corner for five minutes. Think about why you have overdrawn your account (fourth time, really? Are you that irresponsible?).

You probably didn't have an eye on money matters since this was your fourth self-defecation. That's right, you have taken a supreme shit on yourself. I hope you're not proud of this fiasco because it will cost you. The banks like making money as much as you and I do.

When you overdraft your funds and defecate upon your freedom fighters, then you are borrowing the bank's money to pay for your transactions. I'm sure they would let this go on for a while, stacking up hefty fees for every purchase, be it a Coke or a flat-screen TV—size doesn't really matter, especially when it's the bank's money being used.

The bank, being the outstanding financial establishment it is, expects its customers to make smart financial decisions concerning their money. These ideal customers are like persistent hawks who see every transaction and know the exact cash position of all their accounts.

The problem is that most people are horrible managers and overseers of their money. They can earn a fifteen-hundred-dollar-a week paycheck, but by the Thursday of next week, they're back to being broke. Have you ever seen a hamster on a wheel? They're running but not gaining any ground at all.

I used to have this problem myself, caused by a mixture of a low-paying job, bad habits, big dreams, and always a paycheck away from being broke. I eradicated most of that problem when I made a change in my life and went offshore. Still far from perfect, but a lot smarter than I was a few years ago.

Solution: Conscious Money Management

If you have money problems, then read personal finance books, check the Web for blogs written by entrepreneurs and millionaires—get inspired by something and take action. Do whatever you need to do to become a financially educated person. If you bought and read this book, you are taking a step in the right direction. Applying the information given is the next step.

Start managing your own money and disciplining your spending habits. Don't give your paycheck to your mom or significant other and assume that person will do a better job. Do not take a passive role in your financial future, OK? You have the ability to direct yourself toward any goal, desire, or ambition. Do those things that will bring you a lifetime of rewards.

Formal education will make you a living. Self education will make you a fortune.

—Jim Rohn

You can start today by taking control of your finances. Call up your financial institution and cancel the overdraft protection, which states the bank will loan you money at the interest rates they set should your account fall below zero or "overdraft" (don't expect the bank to call you and let you know you're in negative territory either. Understand that they make their money by lending it, with interest, to people like you and I.) Then start actively managing your accounts. Remember how to balance a checkbook? If not, learn how. It's simple addition and subtraction.

Here's a simple exercise. Grab a clean sheet of paper and make two columns. In the left hand column write down the things you *need* to pay to keep on living—food, water, clothing, and shelter. The right hand column is reserved for the things you *want* but do not immediately *need* to sustain your life.

Take your time with this exercise and you will see that the left column contains a few of the items from the list on page thirty-five. It is clear cut, simple, and rather boring, hence the desire to endlessly create exciting new items for the right column. It's way more exciting to talk about a new phone than to talk about paying last month's power bill.

Next to each item in the list, write the price expected for the service, product, or good. Now add up the totals in each of the columns. If you did well with this exercise, you will find the left column shouldn't break the bank by any means. These are your revolving expenses. Keep your focus on it and not so much the right column.

This calls for the art of discipline and unfortunately that is a subject better taught through one's one experience. Is there any room for improvement? Let me go ahead and answer that question for you by saying there is *always* room for improvement.

Set up a savings account that automatically withdraws 10 to 30 percent of your weekly income out of your checking account. That way you will never be stuck in a snowstorm without a shovel. There is no excuse for the person who doesn't try to save any money at all. Make it automatic and forget about it for as long as you have steady income rolling in, which should be your main focus: creating streams of wealth.

If your job pays you twelve dollars an hour, then how can you possibly make any more than that capped rate? Even with overtime, there is a ceiling on your pay rate and the taxman will make his rounds before you see any green. My solution for anyone who doesn't make enough on the job is to invest in something part-time.

Listen carefully to the words that just came out of your mouth, "I don't make enough money at my job." The solution lies outside your job if you can't make enough money there. Somewhere in that other sixteen hours of your day should be a slot of time set aside for your part time business or idea. How does a book or movie get completed? One sentence or frame at a time.

Take a piece of paper and write down all the skills you have acquired in your lifetime, whatever they may be. How many people do you know that could use some of these skills? Maybe you agree to paint a friend's barn for three hundred dollars cash, and you get it done in about four hours. That's equivalent to making seventy-five dollars an hour!

Money From Mistakes?

I'll share a story with you and also the idea that grew from it. In May of 2009, after knocking back a few cold ones one night at a buddy's apartment I hit the road as usual and made my way home. I was pulled over later for doing sixty in a forty mph zone. The field sobriety test was a joke. I failed it miserably and to be honest I'm not sure if sober and coordinated people could pull those stunts off with ease.

To make a long story short, my DUI got thrown out of court after the breathalyzer results revealed I was, in fact, below the legal limit (While I can't justify my actions, I do feel better saying this.) I still got to enjoy all the advantages of being arrested for it though—probation, community service, Alcoholics Anonymous meetings (Not so anonymous anymore, now am I?) and in my state, a mandatory eight hours jail time to sober up.

I don't tell you these things to shock you, but rather to let you know that I'm not a perfect human being and have made my share of mistakes. I continue to learn everyday I am alive and breathing, a persistent pupil of life.

The flipside to this story is the idea I was able to develop from this fiasco in my personal life. There are many people, both young and old, who enjoy going out, socializing, and drinking till the wee hours of the morning. What if they've had too much booze? What are they to do—risk driving home, endangering their lives and the lives of innocent people around them? It's just not worth it.

In the town in which I live, we have certain spots that are more prone to alcoholic activity than others (downtown, near college campuses, concerts). My idea was to have a transit that ran through the hot spots during the prime activity hours offering rides for a reasonable rate and if a customer lived within a thirty mile radius we would even arrange for a small pickup fee or you could pay in advance for round trip service.

This service would be utilized in a large, comfortable bus with A/C and it's fueled by natural gas like the public transit buses you see inside the city limits (if you live in a city that has them), but is very different once inside the swinging doors. My service—the Sobering Gladwagon—is decked out on the inside with flat screen TVs, surround sound, plush seating, and we offer bottled water, juice, and soda for a minimal price.

Can you see my idea? It may or may not work in your individual city. I thought it would work in mine but it's just an idea I had one day while driving around town. I've thought about it and dreamed about it but haven't taken any real action towards it and action, my friends, is the only way I know of to retrieve money from your ideas.

Problem #2

"Looks like I'm on the broke train yet again."

Let me ask you a question. Why in the hell did you get on board in the first place? Wouldn't it have been smarter to hop aboard the Amtrak that leads to success and riches? Being broke is a choice. You either accept it or you don't. The people who don't accept "broke status" get out there and make money. They never enjoyed being broke and won't accept it for themselves or their families.

At the beginning of this book, I told you to direct your mind toward that thing you want most in this life. Don't sit here and tell me that you can't come up with several different approaches to getting off that dreadful locomotive. Many ideas have been offered in these pages, and I've been waiting for the right person to come along and snatch any of them up.

If you are broke, then figure out a way to make money. Don't depend on someone else to bail you out during hard times. What happens when the United States needs money? Word is given to the Treasury and the printers go to work and the giant rollers begin spinning out Jacksons and Benjamins by the sheets. I bet the workers there live under a microscope.

Turn the declarative statement, "Man, I'm like, really broke right now" into an interrogative format: *"How can I make extra money to avoid the ominous broke train?"* The solution lies within the answer to that question.

Problem #3

"How are we going to pay the rent?"

Landlords. I bet that one word stirs up an array of images in your mind. What do you think of? Habitual bitching and nagging, enforced laws that make no sense to you, and, of course, a cocky attitude at all times.

The first of the month rolls around and you, once again, reluctantly pay your dues like clockwork. The landlord on the other hand, is happy and smiling when he sees you've come to pay the rent. Why shouldn't he be happy? This is the reward for his investment. He has earned the right to that check by offering you the most basic of all human needs: shelter.

So get over any bitter feelings or resentment toward your landlord. If anything, I would probe his mind for clues on how to be the one receiving the check, rather than disbursing it. He's a wealth of information, waiting for the right ears to hear his story.

Many will say, "I wish I could be as lucky as that guy." Others become intrigued and will ask, "What is he doing, and what has he done to be so damn successful in his life?" A select few will devote their efforts. "I'm going to model his actions and behaviors until I can produce results like his, and I will never give up until I have reached this objective."

The last group is sure to win because those in it do not recognize failure, only temporary defeat. Call them overachievers or whatever you like, but these people have applied persistence to their goals, knowing they can have whatever they desire in life, no matter how big or ludicrous an idea. If people didn't have ludicrous imaginations, the world would never have seen skyscrapers, theme parks, or airplanes that circle the globe around the clock.

Solution: Getting Your Priorities in Order

Let's say I needed to pay the rent and didn't have the entire amount. I would first go and explain my dilemma to the landlord or property manager. Maybe you can work out a financing plan to help you catch up on payments. It is more cost effective for them to work with tardy renters then it is to paint, clean, and perform any maintenance *prior* to finding another tenant to sign a lease.

The main idea is to take action immediately. Not tomorrow or one day soon. Right fricking now. Don't fret over your problems. Solve them as quickly as possible so you can use your brainpower for more lucrative ventures or passageways. Who wants to sit around and brood over the situation?

Borrow money from a friend or relative (with full intention to pay your debt back promptly), sell your used stuff on eBay/Amazon/Craiglist. As a last resort, you may consider a small payday advance, although I do NOT recommend this solution as they have interest rates in some states that will make you cringe!

Do something so you won't find yourself with a barren bank account and then actively take steps to ensure the problem doesn't happen again. The question is: What are you willing to sacrifice to pay your dues? You won't escape paying bills, but you can escape mediocrity and being consistently broke all the time.

Did you know that Jeff Bezos, the genius behind Amazon's creation, started out in his garage with an idea to sell used books via the World

Wide Web? Amazon has certainly come a long way since its inception. All it takes to be rich is one simple idea, backed by your enthusiasm and perseverance.

Make sure you pay all your debts in a timely manner. Do you think rich people sit around and fret over paying their bills? Hell no, they have a solution for any problem that might arise and the habit of making up their minds quickly and effectively—they do not vacillate in indecision. They move forward with confidence and ease. Their steps are followed by faith and courage as they move forward and progress with their goals.

Problem #4

"Man, I'm so sleepy."

You often hear this complaint almost anywhere you go. Work, school, church, Christmas parties, convenient stores, insomniac circles, etc. The complaint is one of those slight annoyances that you have probably taken part in yourself. I know that I'm guilty here.

I've read stories about professional athletes who sleep ten to twelve hours a night. It's obvious that sleep is important for them to stay alert and focused, and for operating at full potential. They train and push themselves to be the best at their sport. Where do you think their motivation and desire comes from? Role models, parents, coaches, loving spouses?

More than likely, it comes from all of these sources and more, including their own inner desire to win and be the best. First, these athletes realize their natural abilities for their chosen sports. They cultivate these talents and become stronger as their abilities soar to new heights. Secondly, somebody spotted the potential behind the athlete. Maybe they start working together and now both people can sail to new islands of discovery.

The athlete knows they wouldn't have made it this far without the encouragement of positive people in their lives. So they constantly look for more positive and self-driven people with whom to surround themselves. Another alliance has begun.

Solution: Get Some Sleep or Shut Up and Drink a Red Bull!

Dreams keep winners going. These nocturnal warriors can rest six and seven hours a night and feel rejuvenated in the morning because their desire is burning red hot with passion, love, and creativity. If you feel that you need more sleep, then start taking naps more often. Otherwise, shut up and drink a cup of coffee or enjoy an energy drink so you can stay focused and not waste your breath uttering trivialities that really amount to excuses.

If you're driving to the same humdrum job every day and punching the clock, maybe it's your job or the people you are surrounded by that bring you down. Here's an idea. Quit. Yes, march right into that cozy little office and hand over your two weeks' notice (If you are polite and not a jackass—if not, just go ahead and state your resignation. Finished. Try bye.) You can exit stage left and escort yourself out of the miserable confines of a job. But wait a second. There seems to be a problem…

The means of providing your income has been severed and you are on your own. You'll have ample opportunity to catch up on your sleep. Go ahead and get all those pleasant naps in and enjoy happy hour down at your favorite bar. Since your schedule has opened up with a multitude of spare time to fill, work on something that provides a check, electronic deposit, or cash-in-hand for services or products rendered.

As I finish writing this book, it is June 2013. The technology that surrounds us is extraordinary and only seems to get more ridiculous as demand heightens for new products. Seventy-inch high-def televisions, tablets, laptops, Kindles, Web design and programming, app design, video game programming, major motion pictures in 3-D and Imax, refrigerators with TVs. Where does it end?

A lot of you have probably created a website and not even known you were capable of doing such. Remember MySpace, once the king of social networks? If you have ever created a profile, then you've created a webpage. Remember all those codes you copied and pasted in your "About Me" section? That was designed for the computer to read and translate into graphics and text for our viewing pleasure.

If you want to design a website to sell a product or promote your ideas, there is a plethora of books and articles on how to get started. The big bucks are in store for the person who can fill a need via the Internet. The potential reach of the Web is global so you are more likely to catch some really big fish!

I know I could definitely use a refresher course in computer applications. When I took the class, I learned a lot about different programs (Access, Excel, Word, MS-DOS) and their applications. It's only been eight years since I first attended college. My God, where has the time gone? As for sleep, I will leave you with this quote:

If you can't sleep, then get up and do something instead of lying there worrying. It's the worry that gets you, not the lack of sleep.

—Dale Carnegie

VIII. BACK TO THAT

FIRST BIT...

The one thing that offends me the most is when I walk by a
bank and see ads trying to convince people to take out second
mortgages on their home so they can go on vacation. That's
approaching evil.

—Jeff Bezos

Caveat Emptor—You Assume the Risk

Meanwhile back at the ranch...I got off course during the last chapter and I want to make sure I cover all the relevant details when you become serious about purchasing a house. I read a book about flipping properties way before I invested, and the author actually suggested *not* investing in real estate while in your 20s because you make so many different career changes, blah, blah, etc. Needless to say, I didn't follow that guy's advice.

Remember I mentioned that bit about having a notepad and pen on you at all times when scouting for houses to buy? This is absolutely critical to your endeavors in getting the best deal possible on a potential investment.

By now you should be familiarized with the fundamental structure and working systems of a house. Do the faucets work? Is there a large hole in the sheetrock? Termite damage? Is there a mold problem? Does the A/C unit work? How old is it? How old is the house? Is the foundation cracked or sinking? Is the house built on piers?

You'll want to check these things out for yourself. When you are serious about buying and your bid is in to the bank, then the mortgage company will likely want a professional appraiser to assess your property for current value in the market. When you know for sure this is the house you want, then *you* will hire a professional inspector to check the property out and write up a detailed report on the house and its systems and potential problems.

I think I paid my inspector around two hundred dollars and got a seventy-six page report, complete with full-color photos and a written description of what was going on in and around the house. To me this was a minimal price for finding anything I might have missed. After all, it was my money on the line and I wanted to protect my investment.

Preparing For Your Amortization—Wait, What's That?

It's really just a fancy word used to describe the process of paying your debts down over a specific period of time. When you have made your list of possible issues with the property, then you are prepared to make an offer and present it to the bank or owner. You and your realtor will talk over the purchase agreement, making whatever adjustments are needed for your particular case.

Will the seller agree to pay the closing costs or a portion thereof? Will there be a termite bond issued for the property? What kind of mortgage will you use, a traditional thirty-year fixed? The variety of ways to write up an offer on a home is left to your imagination. Have some idea of what you plan to do with the provisions in the agreement. Remember that nothing is final until you sign your name on the dotted line at the closing table.

Different Types of Mortgages—What Suits You Best?

Traditional Thirty-Year Fixed

When we say this mortgage is fixed, that means the interest rate has been locked in at the time of purchase and will not change unless you choose to refinance. This is the option most often used by home buyers, because most people *plan* to keep their homes for thirty years.

If you are an investor, you can take advantage of the lower monthly payments, leveraging your money. You will also be much delighted to know that you can itemize deductions on a primary residence such as interest paid on the mortgage and property taxes when tax season rolls around.

When the first statement arrives in the mailbox, you'll notice your payment is mostly interest with very little principal. It's a thirty-year loan for crying out loud. If you pay it off in the maximum amount of time given—thirty years—you will spend a substantial amount of money paying back the interest of the loan, and that's on top of the original purchase price.

The bank also offers fixed-rate fifteen- and ten- year mortgages in case you like an accelerated debt repayment system. If interest rates drop below the rate you lock in when purchasing, then you can refinance the mortgage at a later date if it should prove beneficial to you.

Adjustable Rate Mortgages

These are trickier mortgages, which are much more personalized for the buyer's needs and agenda. Some examples:

10/1 ARM

What this boils down to is an initial interest rate that is fixed for the first ten years of the loan. After that ten years is up, the rate will adjust to market rates for the remainder of the loan.

5/1, 5/5 ARM

Here the rate will not change for five years. When that sixth year rolls around, the rate will adjust every year for the 5/1 ARM and every five years for the 5/5 ARM.

More Options? Are You Kidding Me?

There are other types of mortgages: 3/3 ARM, 3/1 ARM, balloon mortgages, two-step mortgages, FHA (Federal Housing Administration) loans, and VA (U.S. Department of Veteran Affairs) loans if you are an eligible American veteran. Find one that fits your style and investment plan. Here's a website from Zillow to compare some of the pros and cons of the different options available: www.zillow.com/mortgage/help/Types-Of-Mortgages-And-Home-Loans.htm.

Some options will fit your needs and others may not. When I first started scouting houses, I was considering a FHA loan but found they won't finance homes unless they consider the property livable (For example: the home must have at least one operating bathroom. When you're looking for a flip project, the prospects aren't always in the best of condition.) Talk to a mortgage broker about your individual situation and investment needs.

If you plan to reside in the house for thirty years, then go with the thirty-year fixed route. You can always pay it off quicker. Some mortgage companies include a penalty for prepayment so make sure you read over agreements and contracts carefully before signing any document.

If you're an investor with certain goals for the property—renting to tenants, flipping for cash—then one of the other options may be more suited to your needs. There will be a lot of time to think over your purchase so I recommend jotting your ideas down on paper.

You have now come a long ways, fellow traveler. You have:

☑ Established a good credit rating/score (looking healthy to potential lenders and investors. More info in the next chapter)

☑ Been preapproved by a reputable bank or mortgage company

☑ Secured the funds for your investment (bank account or investor pool)

☑ Found a knowledgeable realtor in your area

☑ Scouted thousands of homes online. Visited several properties and made several offers before finding the best one.

Finding the Right One and Making it Shine

Then do you know what happens? You find the house you really believe has the potential to be something great. It's already something good, but with your talents, it can be a magnificent and welcoming home for others. What you are looking for is the worst house in the best neighborhoods—not the other way around.

Just because something is cheap doesn't mean it's a steal. Ask yourself why they would sell such a goldmine at a ridiculously low price. If you buy the best house in the worst neighborhoods, you may never escape your investment at a favorable price—or at any price at all! In other words, no one will want what you are selling, and you may become stuck with it for an excruciating amount of time.

It isn't as important to buy as cheap as possible as it is to buy at the right time.

—Jesse Livermore

If the location is ideal and the community is growing, then find the worst house in the best areas and solve its problems or nuances before someone else beats you to it. I made a bid on a house that had just come on the market one Friday afternoon. When I looked at the house the following Sunday and made my bid, my realtor said there were already nine other bids in besides mine! The person who won the bid paid more in cash than the original asking price—cash-paying customers always move to the front of the line.

Update that ugly popcorn texture on the ceiling with a flat look and recessed lighting (Keep in mind that some homes built in the 1980s and older, may have used building materials containing asbestos. You will want to have the material examined before undertaking any work and risking health problems and costly removal fees. Also, as a rule of thumb, houses built before 1978 may contain lead paint. Your due diligence phase should catch these things before making any offers.) Install new, shiny appliances. Add a new mailbox and modern landscaping with solar lights around your home. It's the simple things that make a big difference to people.

Attention to detail is important. Go and look at open houses—you can confiscate a lot of ideas from the higher-end homes on the market. See what designs and ideas they have used in their homes that can drive the perceived value higher. Figure out what people are dying to have in their homes and provide it, eloquently.

Crown molding, hardwood floors, travertine tile, chair rail, recessed lighting, under cabinet lighting, Lazy Susans, ceiling fans with remotes, built-in Wi-Fi and sound, textured walls—orange peel, knockdown—operating doorbell, pocket doors, walk-in showers and closets, exterior lights, landscaping, French doors, new cabinet hardware, and, of course, everyone's favorite: granite countertops.

In a modern world, people like updated and hip styles in their homes—this is how you dazzle your customers and instigate their emotions. The house has to feel like home to them, someplace they can stay for a while and not worry about getting robbed. Ask yourself if you would let *your* own kids run around the neighborhood unsupervised.

I have read that most home buyers make a decision in less than a minute about whether they would buy or not. They either love it or they don't. The most important thing you should worry about is how to make your house or investment shine above the other competition out there. If you can create a positive emotional response in a potential home buyer, then you might find yourself signing the deed over to them tomorrow!

What I like to imagine is a couple who is looking for a nice place to settle down and have children. The emotional response should first register in the woman, who is accustomed to displaying beauty and loving warmth in her abode. Her house will speak volumes of her character. The man, on the other hand, just wants to make sure she is happy and comfortable, and he will do whatever possible to please his love, sometimes even jumping off into the American Dream.

You are the producer though, remember? This entitles you the duty and responsibility to provide for the consumers of the world. Your investment has now become a finished product, completely customized for your specific audience. The lovely couple stops by to look at the warm and inviting home you have up for sale. By now, the house has been staged with nice furnishings and a bona fide experience is waiting to happen. Just imagine it.

Dictate Choice: Believe Half of What You Hear or Have None of What You See

Please! Dear God, don't listen to the rambling idiots when they talk about the housing crisis, the real estate market not making a turn around, or how the sky is falling at alarming rates. The amount of advice given today is astounding, and most of the people giving it are completely ignorant or strangely misguided—that's just my opinion.

When someone freely gives their advice, watch out. If you had asked for it, would it not be more valuable? You would really be listening if you had asked someone of their knowledge or advice.

In all probability, you will hear a copious amount of real estate and business advice when venturing down your path toward success. I guess that's how some human beings respond when you tell them you are buying a house or are interested in doing something besides working a dead-end job for thirty years.

They feel the need to connect to the conversation in some way and contribute their two cents of advice, which can sometimes come out sounding like idiot babble, which it could possibly be. I can only think that these people feel like gurus or brainiac philosophers in conversation because they are so thoroughly informed about the nation's affairs vicariously through the media (who are unbiased, right?).

It's typically the kind of inane shit you might pick up by watching the news or reading the paper—and the joke is on them for the amount of time they have invested in believing in and then spreading the garbage in a passionate rant to unsuspecting victims. Who do you think owns the TV stations, networks, and major publishing outlets? That's right, rich people do.

What you get with the news is mainly garbage with an occasional cleverly written article or TV spot, and then more garbage—stories of murders, Ponzi schemes, corruption, and gossip. Yeah, no thanks—I'll pass. I can find more substance on the back of my Captain Crunch cereal box, you know? At least they have fun games and puzzles.

If you don't read the newspaper, you're uninformed. If you read the newspaper, you're misinformed.
—Mark Twain

Start Looking Right in Front of You

Direct your mind toward whatever you desire. Throw the TV out the front door if you have to motivate yourself to get out in the world and find the answers for yourself. If you watch the news daily, what does this contribute to your life? Is it positive or negative? How much passion do you feel when you watch the news or read the newspaper, and why?

If it's not positive, then you have a busted sewage line looking to infiltrate and contaminate your life, spreading negative thoughts throughout your brain and affecting your body and mental state. Think of yourself as a battery, being charged by the daily regimen of material you absorb through your five senses. Batteries can also malfunction (anxiety, high blood pressure, panic attacks, migraines) and/or explode (stroke, heart attack, spontaneous combustion?) when put under extreme conditions (stress) that challenge its true integrity.

Minding Your Own Business

You are the ultimate investor and manager of your time. You decide what books to read, what shows to watch, and what people to hang around. These are the things that represent your character. Say what you like, but know that your choices will reflect in every aspect of your personal life. To change your life is to change your thought patterns and the habits you have slowly formed over the years. Tear down the walls and start with a new game plan.

Time, particularly yours, should be invested wisely, just like your money. If you had no time left on this plateau of existence, your money wouldn't amount to anything of value for you in the next life. So take a mental note that your time is greater than any amount of money you could possibly earn.

Yes, you are capable of reaching soaring heights and altitudes unfathomed, but if your mind is directed toward personal vendettas and revenge plotting, you will be a loser in the game of life. To win at the game of life is to love and help others, not sabotage them or their efforts.

Plenty of folks seem devoted to the task of bringing others down. They incessantly blame their problems on other people—co-workers, bosses, parents, spouses, or friends. How can *your* problems be blamed on anything besides *your* individual thoughts, actions, and choices?

Irresponsible is a fitting word for these people. Ever heard of it? It's when you lack the mental aptitude to recognize that everything in your life resulted from the action you either *chose* to do or not do. No one else is to blame for your problems. I know that can be a rather intimidating pill to swallow, but think of it as a multivitamin on steroids, one that will amp up the horsepower in your life.

This one action alone can create outstanding results in your life. Take responsibility for your problems and understand that the only real power you possess is the ability to direct your mind to create the life you would like to live. As long as your goals are virtuous and altruistic, I can see no reason why the gods wouldn't shine on you, you crazy diamond.

IX. Talk on Credit and Taxes

All the perplexities, confusion and distress in America arise, not from defects in their Constitution or Confederation, not from want of honor or virtue, so much as from the downright ignorance of the nature of coin, credit and circulation.

—John Adams

Credit 101

If you plan to make any larger purchases—real estate, boats, Porsche, home improvement projects—you may obtain financing through several institutions or hard money lenders. Paying back the principal and interest is usually taken care of by you on a monthly basis.

When you apply for a loan, the lender is entitled to run your credit history and your rating as given by the top three credit agencies: Equifax, Experian, and TransUnion. You can actually obtain one free report a year at: www.annualcreditreport.com

Your credit rating will provide the lender with the necessary information to make a decision about lending you money. The lender has to ascertain your stability as a borrower. Do you pay your bills on time every month? How much of your credit limit have you used? They throw all this data into a computer algorithm and come up with a score called FICO (Fair Isaac Corporation, in case you're interested). Of course they have several different scores and ranges for different types of loans—auto, mortgage, personal loans, etc. Let's use a classic and simple example.

The credit score will typically range from 300 to 850. A rating of 300 means you have horrid money management skills and suck at life. Get your act together! Scores of 850 are the epitome of an astute and outstanding citizen. This person's pays bills early and often pays more than the minimum payment. Finances are a day in the park for them.

I'm ashamed to tell you that the average FICO score for my home state of Alabama (scores are pulled from www.credit-report-101.com/average-fico-score.html) was 625 as of November 2012. Not as ashamed as Mississippi should be though. They have claimed the title of lowest credit score in the nation with a 617, not far from Arizona (627) or Louisiana (624).

The median score for the United States is 723 and has been for a few years running. You've probably heard the gurus or talking heads speak of the average US household debt typically being more than ten thousand dollars. Anybody who is paying back student loans or graduate school fees probably has much more debt than that. Think fifty to a hundred thousand dollars. Geez! That could be a mortgage.

What If I've Paid Cash for Everything and Have No Credit?

Yes I've been there too. I mentioned paying off all my debts earlier in the book, remember? One of the things the lady at the bank also mentioned was asking someone with a good credit rating to put me on their account as an authorized user.

If this person has good credit and makes payments on time, then you get partial credit for their good name and credit standing. This goes for the reverse as well. If you don't check the person out well enough and they decide to botch their credit at a later date, it has the possibility of showing up on your credit report. Luckily if you catch this information dragging down your score, you can contact the creditors and request to be removed from the account.

My dad has always been a responsible credit card user and put me on his account. After this action and the revolving payments I automatically made on the secured bank loan, it took about five to six months for my mailbox to start receiving those preapproved credit card offers in the mail.

Pretty soon, I was throwing away offers every week until I found one that was offering $200 FREE dollars if you made $500 in purchases within the first three months. Hold on a second…you mean FREE money? Yeah, I'll take that. I made purchases like groceries, gas, and home improvement items— things I was going to be purchasing anyways.

This is the responsible use of credit. The irresponsible use of credit is buying vanity products, such as designer clothes and shoes, electronics, jewelry, body art and making only the minimum payment with a 15.99 % or higher *variable* interest rate. As a rule of thumb, don't pay on credit unless you:

a.) have the money in the bank and can do without it or

b.) fully believe in your abilities to create and acquire that money within the next month's time frame.

Debt Ceilings and Tax Solutions

The US Treasury Department officially reached the statutory debt limit on Monday, December 31, 2012 (The CNBC app alerted me of that information when I was writing the first draft of this book!). That number is 16.394 trillion dollars. Quite the bar they have set for themselves, don't you think?

On May 10th, 2013, United States Treasury Secretary Jack Lew said the debt ceiling wouldn't be reached until Labor Day and motioned that Congress should deal with the issue right away. I'm beginning to wonder if they will ever solve this problem and stop providing only "temporary solutions."

It is absolutely critical to your success that you strive to do better each and every day and that contribution has to be more than a good-paying job with benefits and a tax-deferred 401(k) plan. These alone will not get you to the top. You will have to become more involved and have a persistent entrepreneurial spirit to escape the rat race.

I'm pretty sure Christopher Columbus did not discover America so we could all hold tight to jobs and slowly build our 401(k)s (Retirement Plans).

—Loral Langemeier, *Put More Cash in Your Pocket*

Instead of filling your head with reality TV, do something productive. Build a website just to see if you can. Set a goal that is so wild and lofty that if you did achieve it, it would flood your bank accounts. Remember that your bank account only reflects the number of people you have helped or served in some way.

If you neglect the advice I have given, then you will grow more dependent upon your job and present environment. You can pay the bills with a job, but with a creative side endeavor—something you have a passion for—you may find your road to financial freedom so you can enjoy retirement while you are still young.

I see no slack in the tax burden upon Americans, particularly the middle class, unless we have a sensible, greedless government in position. At the end of the day, when you realize you aren't capable of controlling your government or leaders, you can take solace from the fact that *you are* in control of your financial well-being, choices, actions, and beliefs.

Facing the Facts

Our very own Constitution gave the federal government the authorization to collect taxes or what they called tariffs way back in those early days. The United States saw the first personal income tax by way of the Revenue Act of 1861, as a way to finance the American Civil War.

It lapsed after the war was over and subsequently came back around with the Revenue Act of 1913, when the government wised up and taxed "all income from whatever source derived." It's right there in the Sixteenth Amendment if you would like to read it for yourself. Wall Street profits were almost safe until that point and so were other sources of capital gains—like real estate or inheritance.

If you plan to stick it out as an employee for a while, count on federal and state taxes increasing as you get older. Mine already have. As of January 1, 2013, the temporary payroll tax cut was eliminated. It was at 4.2 percent, and is now back to 6.2 percent. Your employer matches the 6.2 percent, so it's actually a 12.4 percent contribution, skimmed right off the top!

Remember that 16.394 trillion dollar debt? It will be paid for, in part, by your federal tax contribution, which can jump anywhere from ten to 39.6 percent, depending on your tax bracket and filing status. I've read that the 39.6 percent tax rate was enacted as part of the fiscal-cliff solution, a way for the wealthy to pay more in taxes because they have more to give.

What the wealthy also know is how to protect their assets and grow money trees from seedlings. The seedlings are that extra money you can make and save—put it back, and watch it grow. Not only are you working for money, but money is working for you, growing and multiplying. Only you have the power to control your life's direction and purpose. If you don't sow any seeds, how can you expect to reap any harvest?

All that anyone can see anymore is the finished product, as though it didn't take time and effort to create. I have read that Leo Tolstoy wrote at least seven complete manuscripts of *War and Peace*, all in longhand (It's a behemoth, around 1,200 pages in length.) Maybe that's why scholars have motioned to call the book one of the most important works of world literature.

Lasting success comes only through planning and execution. It comes from sheer hard work, the result of which should be enjoyed and respected, since it is directed toward receiving the fulfillment of one's innermost dream.

—Nicolas Darvas, *The Anatomy of Success*

X. Good Advice is Always Free

Wise men don't need advice. Fools won't take it.
—Benjamin Franklin

Valuable Advice is Found Through Trial and Error

Happiness, health, and wealth. That sums it up in a nutshell, doesn't it? At least for the most part. This is what most people are searching for. Scan the *New York Times* nonfiction best-sellers list and you'll understand that people want to know about these three things and how to achieve them.

We have one author saying, "Be wise with your money and skip out on the grande mocha latte." Yet another says to indulge in your tastes, don't overdo it, but don't deny yourself the right. It is easy to be whipsawed by different people's formulas for wealth. You won't follow everybody's advice but will pick and choose what fits your lifestyle and investment approach. Don't read one book and think you have done something. Read a hundred and then you get to brag.

There are thousands of books, audio books, and videos written and produced by talented people who achieved personal success. Study their stories and analyze their individual formulas for wealth creation to see if you can apply any of their knowledge to your own financial plan. Knowledge only becomes power when used and directed toward an objective.

Your mind needs to be saturated with success, wealth, happiness, love, understanding, and reason. You can fill your entire room with books concerning success and personal finance, but unless you read and apply the knowledge, then change will not endure.

Experience is where the real lessons are taught. Reading about others' experiences can assist you in building and maintaining your own success. It will help to familiarize your with the terms and common instances in whatever profession or goal you seek.

In the twenty-first century, we have no excuse for not having whatever we desire. Think of the triumphs of Henry Ford, Thomas Edison, John D. Rockefeller, and Andrew Carnegie. They had no instruction manuals and no Internet, just a burning desire to realize the biggest dreams possible.

Poverty will accept damn near anyone, but riches have a particular code for their acquisition. You must follow certain rules and procedures that most people either don't know or don't take the time to hear. They have their own stack of problems at home.

Millionaire Status

Wealth comes from knowing what others do not know.
—Aristotle Onassis, Greek shipping magnate

The majority of millionaires today are self-made, products of their own creation—no inheritance passed down, no golden lottery ticket in hand. Becoming a millionaire by your own hand gives you the appreciation for the hard-earned money you have saved so diligently. Many people—perhaps your parents even—make millions over the course of their lives, but how much of it do they save?

To be considered a millionaire really translates into having a net worth of one million dollars—that is, the sum of the value of all your assets, cash accounts, and liquid investments. Get on the right train of thought financially and you can spend your time enjoying the beach in your young, fit body.

You could spend ten to fifteen years working hard for someone else's business or spend that same amount of time building something that will pay you dividends on a regular basis over the course of your life. Only you possess the choice to spend your life as you see fit.

Everything you do is a choice. Maybe you work forty hours a week and bring home a steady, but small, paycheck. Maybe you collect unemployment and sell your crazy pill prescriptions to pay the rent. We all trade something of value for another.

A lot of people hold the belief that rich people are bad, that they probably crossed somebody or stole their way to the top. No no no! What they did was wake up and take control of their lives. They came out of the dugout swinging hard, setting goals, and following through with them until they achieved that for which they aimed. That isn't a bad person—that's an inspiration! This doesn't imply the logic that all rich people are good people.

All the rich people I've had the gracious opportunity of meeting are friendly, polite, and generally easy to talk to. They understand and have a real passion for humanity. Being a millionaire has opened their eyes to see beyond the realm of unpaid bills and debt collectors. They set their minds free from that pile of garbage a long time ago, perhaps because they knew there is more to life than, "How am I going to pay the rent?"

Once they realized having riches was mandatory in pursuing their true dreams and passions, then they set out to correct their money problems and free up their precious time. They asked, "What do the rich do, because they must have done something right."

Once you start to plan your future, you can watch your life grow. You are a person of action, and intelligent thought permeates your being. You don't fret over your problems; you rise to the occasion and answer the call for *action*. Seize it and unfold it.

Law of Attraction in 200 Words or Less

Can you remember a first love or crush when you were younger? Do you remember how it made you feel like you could conquer the world, be anybody, or do anything you wanted? Stop and think about it for a minute. Those feelings were alien to you until you met your crush and developed feelings toward that person.

Maybe you thought of this person regularly and imagined the two of you together kissing or something like that. This mental sabotage grew into a full-time obsession didn't it? Day in and day out, you added more fuel to the fire burning beneath that desire.

What you were doing was attracting the object of your desire by stimulating your imagination with mental images. You cultivated your imagination and set your focus on the prize, never allowing doubt or fear to enter your mind. The mind of a child is uninhibited by these things before adulthood closes in, unless of course you watched *The X-Files* before bedtime.

Intrigue is the essence of captivation.
—J. L. Williams

Health Appreciation

Go into any of your social circles and bring up what you eat. Suddenly everyone is a health expert. No need to worry, I won't keep you long. Here's what I believe on maintaining a healthy body.

Being healthy means not overdoing the consumption level (unless you're eating lettuce or another green vegetable), and you cannot fill your body with garbage food and expect to look like a model. That logic doesn't work. You are what you eat…cliché, I know, but it still holds true.

There will be times to treat yourself but this should never become a habit. Habitual bad eating will get you two thumbs down from me. To be lean is to think more natural products. Bananas, apples, and spinach are my personal favorites (Cholesterol is produced in the liver of animals.) I'm not a vegan, but I do have vegan tendencies at times.

Think more earth and what comes from it. Fresh fruit, vegetables, nuts, and beans, all produced by Mother Nature—not a cheese pizza loaded with fats. That screams indigestion and constipation if the grease doesn't hit your bowels first.

Do you enjoy eating double cheeseburger, extra large combos every day for lunch or do you manage your health like you manage your money? If you are depleting your health status with *habitual* bad habits, extra large combos with diet soda—I'm sure you saved a lot of calories there—formidable beer pong standings, cigarette smoking, etc., then you are likewise killing your time and money in the metaphorical way, like picking up a butcher knife and stabbing at each repeatedly. Why are you killing your time so ceaselessly? It is the biggest asset in your life so why the reproach?

Remember when your parents said to you, "You're going to wish you hadn't done that?" I bet that lit a fuse under your rebellious teenage spirit, didn't it? "Ha, they say I can't do it. Just wait and I'll show them!" What a naïve and unreasonable attitude. Some would say the logic and reasoning mechanisms have not united in the frontal lobes—scientists say this happens after your early twenties. Perhaps…

Am I saying that you can't enjoy a pizza, eat a cheeseburger, or drink a beer when you like? No I'm not. Eat, drink, and be merry friends! Right now, I have my cheeseburger fix worked down to about two days a week and that is usually done on the weekends when I feel like rewarding myself for the week's hard work. But I know better than eating those delicious burgers all the time. One it's costly and two, just like a played out pop song, it loses its value when it goes viral on you.

Disclaimer

I'm no health expert—or any expert at all, for that matter. I am someone who is interested in changing my life for the better, in any way that correlates with being successful. This is a lifelong pursuit that I have planned. Who's to say where the peak of my success will be? No one but I.

Yeah, but my Uncle Homer from Timbuktu said that he tried that idea out and it was a giant failure. I say, what the hell do they know, and why have you deemed this person so relevant to your life as to sway your decision to keep moving forward?

I certainly love good advice, and sometimes it can be really valuable information. The question to answer is: What is the track record of this person? Do they know what they are talking about? Are they wealthy? Successful in any one way? Or are they broke and living under a pile of massive debt, barely capable of keeping up with the payments?

If we had good advice police to enforce the laws and ask those important questions, we could easily verify whether this person is the real deal or just some hackbag blowing smoke up our ass.

XII. Conclusion

I don't know of any first class airfare that will escort you to the land of wealth. Unless your father is the pilot, you're stuck in the back with everybody else.

—J. L. Williams

You've Got the Rope Now! Welcome to the End of All Excuses!

Here we are at the end of our come-to-Jesus meeting. We'll be parting ways soon, and I hope this book lingers in your head for a while, or maybe you feel spontaneous and want to read it again. Remember that no matter the obstacle or hurdle, you can leap over it and you can live the life you always dreamed of, provided you are prepared to pay the price for its attainment.

What are you willing to sacrifice today for a more luxurious tomorrow? Are you willing to cut off the cable or satellite connection so you have an excuse to read and study more educational books and programs? Can you do without those three-hundred-dollar sunglasses right now?

Am I saying you have to live frugally? Absolutely not. In fact, frugality shouldn't be your focus when you are aspiring to attain wealth—it can assist you in saving money, but you should be more concerned with creating numerous streams of income to supplement your dreams and goals.

There are several personal finance books on the shelves today, many of which top best-seller lists, that can help you or possibly lead you down a primrose path of uncertainty. Beware of those gurus! Read several books before you form an opinion of how different people have attained great wealth in this country.

Do they practice what they preach? How did they make it to millions? Was it the royalties from their best-selling book, or did they really embrace phenomenal wealth after cutting coupons for five years? I'm cheap myself, but I don't generally take the time to cut coupons—not to knock any of their advice or anyone who follows it. I've found some has value, but not all of it is necessarily going to match every person's individual needs.

Anyone who has acquired wealth has followed a formula, and that formula can be modeled and modified for your personal belief systems. It's not rocket science to get rich. All it takes is a sound plan for the attainment of your desire, one in which you are persistent.

Giving up at the first struggle is not an option. Complaining about your personal problems is not an option. Re-think. Re-organize. Try again until you strike gold. Riches will not fall into your lap until you can provide something of significant value to this world many times over. That is a simple enough formula to follow, yes?

This product or service you provide is within you right now, awaiting your acknowledgment. How fast could this idea produce a million dollars? Fifteen million? If you want incredibly fast results, the Internet has helped produce countless millionaires.

Several entrepreneurs have found ways of providing value over the Web—Amazon, Google, Yahoo!, Groupon, Yelp, LinkedIn, Tumblr (26 year old founder David Karp recently sold it to Yahoo! for a price tag of $1.1 billion), Facebook, Twitter, and, of course, who could forget pornography sites?

Many are millionaires, and possibly even billionaires because of the number of people they have exposed their product or service to. The Internet expands the globe so your potential reach is the most efficient for achieving the really big results.

I am interested in Web design and plan to start reading more books on the subject. Where else can you offer your products or services to such a huge audience? I hope that by the time my next book is written (Whereas I established this book as being a *need* in the marketplace, the next one I want to work on the *wants* of readers. Hello fiction!), I can give you some updates on my progress in programming and Web design or have a website to visit.

Many things are on the to-do list this year. As I write this, it is June 4th, 2013, and I realize I started writing this book about five months ago on December 28, 2012. I'm glad I made up my mind to finally finish a book whether I thought I had enough experience or not. What I felt when I started was that I had read enough books in my life to produce and organize one of my own, and the learning experience itself has been most enlightening and becoming of my own personality and character.

It has been supremely fun, and I am delighted that you held my company for a time. I have a feeling we will meet again one day soon. Maybe by then we will have more free time to parlay. Take care and be yourself out there. Don't accept what other people want for your life. You are the captain of the ship, remember? Concentrate on your goals and feed your dreams daily—that's about the best advice you'll ever hear.

What do I mean by concentration? I mean focusing totally on the business at hand and commanding your body to do exactly what you want it to do.

—Arnold Palmer

The knowledge I have gained over the years, I have practiced at my will and discretion, and I hope that the content within these pages has informed you; inspired you; and, above all, made you bellow with laughter. If it has, please tell a friend or email your thoughts and opinions to: j.l.williams1040@gmail.com.

When I make an impromptu visit to the bookstore and open a book that catches my eye, I want to feel something in the words. If that emotion happens to be laughter, then I'm sold on it, hook, line, and sinker. Do you know why? Laughter makes me feel good, and I want to do that which produces those feelings of happiness and well-being.

Live, and for the love of all that is holy, laugh once in a while. Maybe you can sneak in a five-minute laugh riot on your way to work one morning. Perhaps you're already the type of person who laughs out loud, wherever you happen to be, at any given moment. If you're not, I can promise that if you make laughing more in your everyday life a priority, then your problems will look less dismal and you might find you really do love your life. God bless and Godspeed on your personal journey with success.

The pursuit of happiness and knowledge must be ever-present. There is no excuse for not following through. None. Keep your eyes forever upon the burning desire of your being. Feed the fire with the imaginings of your future self and life.

What do you want? Imagine it with every possible detail. Utilize every tool in the toolbox. You must have the probability of success in your favor, so do everything and anything that will bring you closer to the attainment of your desires, no matter how minute you think the task is.

APPENDIX

REAL ESTATE

PURCHASE AGREEMENT

Date 7-11-2011

This contract constitutes the sole agreement between the parties hereto and any modifications of this contract shall be signed by all parties to this agreement. No representation, promise, or inducement not included in this contract shall be binding upon any party hereto. If you have any questions, seek legal and/or tax advice.

AGENCY DISCLOSURE:SELLER(S) INITIALS _____ _____   BUYER(S) INITIALS ___JW___ _____

The listing company _Remax_ is:	The selling company _____ is:
(Two blocks may be checked)	(Two blocks may be checked)
_|An agent of the seller.	_|An agent of the seller.
_|An agent of the buyer.	_|An agent of the buyer.
_|An agent of both the seller and buyer and is acting as a limited consensual dual agent.	_|An agent of both the seller and buyer and is acting as a limited consensual dual agent.
_|Assisting the ____ buyer ____ seller as a transaction broker.	X|Assisting the _x_ buyer ____ seller as a transaction broker.

BUYER'S OFFER DATE 7-11-2011 _____ Am. ____ (AM/PM)

1. THE UNDERSIGNED, HEREINAFTER CALLED THE BUYER, HEREBY OFFERS TO BUY THE PROPERTY LOCATED IN _____
ALABAMA,COMMONLY KNOWN AS _____
AND LEGALLY DESCRIBED AS _Lot 1_
SUBJECT TO ANY EXISTING BUILDING AND USE RESTRICTIONS, PREVIOUS MINERAL EXCLUSIONS, ZONING ORDINANCES AND EASEMENTS, IF ANY, FOR THE SUM OF _Sixty Five Thousand Dollars_ ($ _65,000_)

2. THE TERMS OF THE PURCHASE SHALL BE AS INDICATED BY "X" BELOW, UNMARKED TERMS DO NOT APPLY.

~~CASH~~   _|The full purchase price upon execution and delivery of a full Warranty Deed by the Seller. The Buyer shall pay closing fee and recording fee.

NEW MORTGAGE   X|The full purchase price upon execution and delivery of a full Warranty Deed by the Seller contingent upon the Buyer's ability to obtain a _30_ YEAR _Conv_ TYPE mortgage in the amount of approximately $ _52,000_ PLUS _|PMI, _|MIP, _|VA FUNDING FEE, _|CLOSING COST AT AN INTEREST RATE NOT TO EXCEED _5%_ % or market rate if not locked in at the time of application. The Seller shall have the option to cancel this contract if the Buyer fails to apply for a mortgage loan within _5_ business days after the date of acceptance of this offer. Credit report fee shall be paid by Buyer at time of application and ordered immediately. Appraisal fee shall be paid by Buyer at time of application. Buyer shall direct lender to order appraisal immediately upon receipt of credit report satisfactory to lender and removal of the professional inspection contingency should one apply. THIS OFFER IS CONTINGENT ON THE PROPERTY APPRAISING FOR AT LEAST THE PURCHASE PRICE. The Buyer shall pay all loan closing costs, unless otherwise noted, including prepaid items, unless not allowed by FHA/VA regulations. The Seller shall make repairs or replacements as required by appraisal, or for mortgage loan purposes, NOT TO EXCEED $ _500_ , but not including possible repairs as may be required by paragraphs 4 and 8 below.

~~VENDOR'S LIEN~~   _|$ _____ upon execution and delivery of a full Warranty Deed by the Seller reserving a Vendor's Lien wherein the balance of $ _____ shall be payable in # ____/____ instalments of $ _____ including interest at ____% per annum, the first payment to become due 30 days after _____ . No penalty for prepayment privileges. The Buyer to pay closing fees and recording fee. The Vendor's Lien _|SHALL _|SHALL NOT be assumable without written consent of the lien holder, and the Vendor's Lien/Note _|SHALL _|SHALL NOT contain a late charge provision of ____ % of an installment when paid more than ____ days after due date thereof. Set up fee and note collection fee, if any, to be paid by the _|BUYER _|SELLER. The Vendor's Lien shall require the Buyer to promptly pay ad valorem taxes and to furnish insurance coverage in an amount not less than Vendor's Lien retained on buildings and improvements, with standard mortgagees clause naming the Seller as a loss payee, with the Buyer to supply first year insurance policy at closing. The Buyer _|SHALL _|SHALL NOT provide a credit report satisfactory to and approved in writing by the Seller within ____ business days of the acceptance of this agreement. The Vendor's Lien/Note _|SHALL _|SHALL NOT provide for a balloon payment due _____

3. BUYER IS AWARE THAT PROFESSIONAL INSPECTION(S) , including but not limited to hazardous substances, of home, structure and systems, and any other items of importance to the Buyer are available, by a representative of the Buyer's choosing. The sale X|IS _|IS NOT contingent on said inspection, satisfactory to the Buyer. If sale is contingent on said inspection, the Buyer agrees to pay for same, and if said inspection is found to be unsatisfactory to the Buyer, the Seller is to be notified in writing within _10_ business days of acceptance of this agreement. Otherwise, this contingency will be considered removed at the expiration of such period. The Seller is not obligated to pay for any repairs recommended by such professional inspection, except as may be required by other provisions of this purchase agreement. If this offer is contingent on a professional inspection, the appraisal, if any, shall be ordered immediately upon the removal of this contingency. Buyer has been given the opportunity to have such an inspection and hereby declines _____ BUYER(S) INITIALS.

4. THE BUYER ACCEPTS THIS PROPERTY IN ITS AS IS CONDITION, except as may be specified herein. HEATING, COOLING AND AIR CONDITIONING EQUIPMENT INCLUDING ANY WINDOW UNITS, PLUMBING and ELECTRICAL SYSTEMS and all INCLUDED APPLIANCES shall be warranted by the Seller to be in working order at time of conveyance. Buyer to be responsible for inspection of same prior to conveyance. The Buyer may be requested to sign a final walk-thru/systems check inspection form, indicating that the inspection was completed and that the property was acceptable, unless otherwise noted on such form. The Buyer understands that if Realtor accompanies the Buyer on this final inspection it will be as a courtesy only and not as a person qualified to detect any defects.

5. PROVIDING UTILITY AVAILABILITY, if necessary, for any and all inspections is the responsibility of the _|BUYER X|SELLER.

6. A HOME WARRANTY subject to limitations, exclusions and deductibles X|SHALL _|SHALL NOT be provided. If provided, Home Warranty shall be ordered by _____ Realtors through _Old Republic_ Warranty Company at the expense of _|BUYER X|SELLER. Buyer has been given the opportunity to have such coverage and hereby declines _____ BUYER(S) INITIALS.

7. ALL IMPROVEMENTS AND APPURTENANCES ARE INCLUDED IN THE PURCHASE PRICE, including if now in or on the property, the following: lighting fixtures and their shades, ceiling fans, drapery hardware and curtain hardware, window shades and blinds, window and door screens, stationary laundry tubs, water heater, smoke detectors, carbon monoxide detectors, built-in security systems, TV antenna, satellite dish, mailbox, remote control garage door opener(s), water pump and pressure tank, built-in kitchen appliances including garbage disposal, central vac attachments, gas logs and related equipment, attached gas grill, awnings, all plantings, and heating and air conditioning equipment including any window units. The Seller shall provide to the buyer or selling broker at closing at least one (1) door key to each separately keyed exterior door of dwelling and outbuilding(s). Exceptions for leased equipment: _____
NO ITEMS OF PERSONAL PROPERTY SHALL BE TRANSFERRED TO THE BUYER UNLESS SPECIFICALLY ITEMIZED HEREIN:
_____

Personal property / free-standing appliances that remain are of NO VALUE for appraisal and mortgage loan purposes unless otherwise noted.

8. THE SELLER AGREES TO FURNISH AT SELLER'S EXPENSE, AN ALABAMA WOOD INFESTATION REPORT from a bonded and licensed termite control company stating that a visual inspection of accessible areas of the dwelling and garage and/or carport and any detached buildings given value by appraisal indicates there is no visible sign of active infestation by wood destroying insects or fungus. This is not a structural damage report nor a warranty as to the absence of wood destroying insects or fungus. If a lender requires a structural inspection due to a finding of previous or present infestation and/or damage, such inspection shall be at Seller's expense and shall be satisfactory to Buyer and lender; or if not required by lender, Buyer may order such structural inspection at Buyer's expense, satisfactory to Buyer. The current termite contract, if any, is to be kept current by the Seller and transferred to the Buyer if allowed by termite company at the expense of the _|BUYER X SELLER at a cost not to exceed $ _180_ . If active infestation and/or fungus is reported, treatment of the entire dwelling may be required unless property is under a current termite contract in which case a re-treatment of the affected area will be permitted. If new construction, a soil treatment letter is acceptable in lieu of inspection. Formosan coverage X SHALL _|SHALL NOT be added to the existing contract if not presently included at the expense of _|BUYER X SELLER. If property is not covered by a termite contract, Seller X SHALL' _|SHALL NOT provide termite replacement coverage X WITH |WITHOUT Formosan coverage at Seller's expense.

SELLER(S) INITIALS _____ _____   BUYER(S) INITIALS _Glal_ _____

REAL ESTATE   REVISED 3-10

Property Address:_____

9. ALL AD VALOREM TAXES, any Homeowners Association Fees, and any rents being collected from existing tenants to be prorated at time of closing. Subject to the terms of any existing lease, the lease agreements and security/damage deposits, if applicable, will be transferred to the Buyer at closing. NOTE: Taxes are prorated based upon current information furnished by the Revenue Commissioner's Office. Realtors cannot and do not assume an responsibility for any change, modification or adjustment to the current tax assessment by the Revenue Commissioner's Office.
10. LIENS FOR PUBLIC IMPROVEMENTS shall be paid by the Seller without proration. Assessments for public improvements not yet a lien shall b assumed by the Buyer.
11. AN OWNER'S POLICY OF TITLE INSURANCE in the amount of the purchase price is to be furnished by the Seller. Risk of loss by fire or othe casualty shall be on the Seller until title is conveyed.
12. A NEW SURVEY shall be paid for by _|BUYER _|SELLER and ordered by _|LISTING BROKER _|SELLING BROKER. Buyer has been given th opportunity to get a new survey and hereby declines _Glw/ BUYER(S) INITIALS.
13. SALE TO BE CLOSED within _3_ days after all necessary documents are ready, no sooner than _8-1_ , _11_ , nor later tha _8-15_ . _11_
TITLE TO BE TAKEN IN THE NAME(S) of _____
_|WITH X WITHOUT Right of Survivorship.
14. A FURTHER PERIOD OF FIVE (5) DAYS shall be allowed for closing if: (A) the closing is delayed by reason of title defects which can be readi corrected, or (B) the terms of purchase requires a new mortgage, and the lender issues an unconditional written commitment no later than the end dat in paragraph 13 above, but is delayed in consummating the mortgage.
15. POSSESSION TO BE GIVEN X AT CLOSE _____ DAYS AFTER CLOSE OF SALE, AT _____ (AM/PM)
_| WITH _| WITHOUT payment of rent by the Seller for any portion of property occupied by the Seller prior to this date and paid a follows:_____
16. THIS OFFER SHALL REMAIN OPEN UNTIL _8 pm_ (am/pm) on _7-13-2011_ , and if not properly accepted an delivered , time is void. Buyer deposits $ _500_ as earnest money to be deposited by the Selling Broker upo acceptance of this offer, cash shall be deposited immediately, and to be applied against the purchase price at closing. If the offer/counteroffer is no accepted, the earnest money shall be returned to Buyer without Seller's signature. If for any reason the transaction is not consummated or if there is disagreement involving to whom the earnest money should be disbursed, Broker is required by law to obtain a written agreement signed by Buyer an Seller before disbursement of earnest money. If such written agreement signed by Buyer and Seller cannot be obtained, Broker may interplead suc funds into court, with Broker's attorneys fees and costs for the interpleader action to be deducted there from. In the event of Buyer's default, Seller ma elect to retain such deposit as liquidated damages or as part payment of the purchase price and pursue Seller's available remedies against the Buyer. I the event of Seller's default, Buyer may pursue available remedies against the Seller.
17. THE PURCHASE PRICE AND TERMS OF THIS SALE MAY BE DISCLOSED after closing to the members and affiliate members of the Mobile Are Association of REALTORS, Inc., or the GULF COAST MLS, INC., or other applicable MLS, for use in the ordinary conduct of their business. REALTOR may benefit financially as a result of recommending real estate related services to clients and customers. REALTORS ARE NOT PRINCIPALS AN ARE NOT TO BE HELD LIABLE FOR ANY CONDITIONS OR NON-PERFORMANCE OF THIS AGREEMENT NOR HAVE THEY GIVEN ANY LEGA OR TAX ADVICE.
18. Seller's Disclosure Statement is acknowledged by BUYER (S) INITIALS and "X" below (other unmarked statements do not apply).
_____ _|Buyer acknowledges and accepts "Seller's Disclosure Statement".
_____ _|This agreement is contingent upon Buyer's written acceptance of "Seller's Disclosure Statement" and return with accepted contract.
Glw X Buyer and Seller agree to waive execution of "Seller's Disclosure Statement".

19. ADDENDUMS INDICATED ARE INCLUDED as part of this agreement: LEAD-BASED PAINT DISCLOSURE _____ , OTHER(S) _____

20. Other provisions: _Seller to contribute $2275 to buyers closing costs, prepaid items and Reserves. Seller to pay up to $399 for home warranty, $180 for W&B and termite bond and appraisal repairs not to exceed $500_

21. THE BUYER ACKNOWLEDGES that Buyer has read this entire agreement including all addendums, if any, which are made part of this purchase agreement and has received copies thereof.

Buyer X _____   Print Name _____

Buyer X _____   Print Name _____

Buyer's Address _____ _____ Phone: _____

Witness X _____ Realtor _____ Phone (Off.) _____ (Other) _____

SELLER'S ACCEPTANCE OF OFFER   Date: _____ , _____ (AM/PM)

22. THE ABOVE OFFER IS HEREBY ACCEPTED _____

IN THE EVENT A COUNTEROFFER is made, it shall expire on _____ , _____ (AM/PM) if the Buyer has not given prior written acceptance. THE SELLER ACKNOWLEDGES that Seller has read this entire agreement including all addendums, if any, which are made part of this purchase agreement and has received copies thereof.

Seller X _____ Print Name _____

                                                As Title is Held
Seller X _____ Print Name _____

Seller's Address _____ Phone: _____

Witness X _____ Realtor _____ Phone (Off.)_____(Other) _____

BUYER'S ACCEPTANCE OF COUNTEROFFER   Date: _____ , _____ (AM/PM)

23. The Seller's counteroffer as detailed in #21 above is hereby _]countered as per attached addendum _]accepted as written. Provisions of the original offer not changed by counters remain in effect.

Buyer X _____ Witness _____

Buyer X _____ Witness _____

FEES WORKSHEET
Fee Details and Summary

Applicants: Rudolph McGrath
Prepared By:

Application No:
Date Prepared: 08/09/2011
Loan Program: 30 year fixed

THIS IS NOT A GOOD FAITH ESTIMATE (GFE). This "Fees Worksheet" is provided for informational purposes ONLY, to assist you in determining an estimate of cash that may be required to close and an estimate of your proposed monthly mortgage payment. Actual charges may be more or less, and your transaction may not involve a fee for every item listed.

Total Loan Amount: $ 54,400   Interest Rate: 4.500 %   Term/Due In: 360 / 360 mths

Fee	Paid To	Paid By (Fee Split)	Amount	PFC	F	POC
ORIGINATION CHARGES						
Loan Origination Fee	Seller	1.000%	$ 544.00	✓	✓	
Administration fee	Seller		$ 595.00	✓	✓	
OTHER CHARGES						
Appraisal Fee	Seller		$ 350.00		✓	
Closing/Escrow Fee	Seller		$ 400.00	✓	✓	
Lender's Policy	Borrower		$ 597.00			
Owner's Title Insurance	Borrower		$ 193.00			
Pest Inspection Fee	Borrower		$ 125.00			
Mortgage Recording Charge	Borrower		$ 76.00			
Transfer Tax	Seller		$ 103.00		✓	
Hazard Insurance Reserves	Borrower	$ 140.00 x 2 mth(s)	$ 280.00			
County Property Tax Reserves	Borrower	$ 39.60 x 2 mth(s)	$ 79.20			
Daily Interest Charges	Borrower	$ 6.8000 x 2 day(s)	$ 13.60	✓		
Hazard Insurance Premium	Borrower	$ 140.00 x 12 mth(s)	$ 1,680.00			

TOTAL ESTIMATED FUNDS NEEDED TO CLOSE				TOTAL ESTIMATED MONTHLY PAYMENT	
Purchase Price (+)	68,000.00	Loan Amount (-)	54,400.00	Principal & Interest	275.64
Alterations (+)		CC Paid by Seller (-)	2,380.00	Other Financing (P & I)	
Land (+)		Seller Paid Title Fees	540.00	Hazard Insurance	140.00
Refi (incl. debts to be paid off) (+)				Real Estate Taxes	39.60
Est. Prepaid Items/Reserves (+)	2,052.80			Mortgage Insurance	
Est. Closing Costs (+)	2,983.00			Homeowner Assn. Dues	
				Other	
Total Estimated Funds needed to close			15,715.80	Total Monthly Payment	455.24

* PFC = Prepaid Finance Charge   F = FHA Allowable Closing Cost   POC = Paid Outside of Closing
** B = Borrower   S = Seller   Br = Broker   L = Lender   TP = Third Party   C = Correspondent

Calyx Form - feews.frm (09/2010)